The Creation of QATAR

The Creation of QATAR

Rosemarie Said Zahlan

R

ROUTLEDGE
London and New York

First published 1979 by Croom Helm Ltd
Reprinted 1989 by Routledge
11 New Fetter Lane, London EC4P 4EE
29 West 35th Street, New York, NY 10001

Printed and bound in Great Britain by
Biddles Ltd, Guildford and King's Lynn

A catalogue record of this book is available
from the British Library.
    ISBN 0-415-03936-3

Library of Congress Cataloging in Publication Data

Zahlan, Rosemarie Said.
    The creation of Qatar.

    Bibliography: p. 148
    Includes index.
    1. Qatar-History. I. Title.
DS247.Q38Z33 1979   953'.63   79-1361
ISBN 0-415-03936-3

CONTENTS

For, of course, ABZ.

KINGDOM OF SAUDI ARABIA

GULF OF OMAN

Muscat

OMAN

IRAN

STRAIT OF HORMUZ

Lingeh

Sharjah

Dubai

UNITED ARAB EMIRATES

Abu Dhabi

THE GULF

QATAR

Doha

BAHRAIN

Hawar Is.

Bushire

Dammam

SAUDI ARABIA

IRAQ

Basra

KUWAIT

ACKNOWLEDGEMENTS

Unpublished Crown Copyright material in the India Office Library and Records and in the Public Record Office transcribed here appear by permission of the Controller of Her Majesty's Stationery Office.

I would like to express my appreciation to a few of the people who contributed to the manuscript. The staff of the India Office Library and Records have always been most generous in their assistance, and here I would like to single out Penelope Tuson for all her efforts. I am also grateful to Marwan Buheiry for his thoughtful and important comments, and to Anna Allen and Sian Thomas for typing the manuscript. As always, it is to my husband, A. B. Zahlan, that I owe most. He gave much of his valuable time to reading and commenting on the text as well as contributing facts and ideas to the final chapter. Any shortcomings that might exist, of course, are entirely my own.

PREFACE

What was undoubtedly the first mention of Qatar in the Western media appeared on 24 January 1935 in the *Daily Express* (Britain). Three days later, a similar article, obviously inspired by the same source, appeared in *The People*. Both articles pictured the ruler of Qatar as a fabulous 'Sheik of Arabia': they gave Arabian Nights accounts of the eighty-odd members of his beautiful harem, his 'piles of pearls', the breathtaking qualities of his court and his romantic country complete with four thousand slaves. Nothing could have been further from reality, as the following pages will clearly illustrate.

Although the articles do not seem to have created more than a ripple of interest outside a restricted circle of British officials, they were in fact a direct outcome of the Anglo-American rivalry that had recently developed over the acquisition of an oil concession in Qatar. The British government, in treaty relations with Qatar, only allowed its ruler to sign a commercial agreement with a British-controlled company. The rival US company retaliated by leaking the information to the press in order to draw attention to the Gulf states in deliberate opposition to the British policy of suppressing all information on the region.

The articles were the last to appear on Qatar in many years. It was only when oil in sizeable quantities began to be exported and when Qatar gradually began to take its place amongst the sovereign states of the world that some literature on it started to reappear. But the reasons for this can once again be linked to Qatar's large petroleum resources, almost as if that fact alone were the *raison d'être* of the small state on the western shores of the Gulf.

There can be no doubt of Qatar's present economic importance. It is a supplier of energy, and its indigenous population has the third highest *per capita* income in the world; in 1978, this figure stood at $11,400 (roughly £5,700) with $2 billion its oil revenue that year, to say nothing of its vast reservoir of associated and unassociated gases.[1] Oil production itself reached over two and a half billion barrels in 1977, practically all of which was exported, the United States being the single largest importer. Over and above these facts, the government of Qatar is in the process of expanding and diversifying its economy. For this, it has to rely heavily on foreign, mostly Western, technology and man-power, skilled and otherwise. Furthermore, until it becomes more

11

self-sufficient, Qatar will have to continue to depend on considerable importation of food and commodities. In 1976 this amounted to approximately $1.3 billion or £650 million[2] for a total population of around 220,000. The bulk of these goods came from Western countries, thus increasing the importance of Qatar to these states.

These statistics amply illustrate Qatar's recent and remarkable prosperity but in themselves they tell us nothing of the structure and maintenance of Qatari society. To date there has been virtually no literature that seeks to understand and explain Qatar's evolution through its history. Such information as exists is scant and not readily available; by and large, it is also unreliable. It is noteworthy that much less has been written on Qatar than on any other Gulf state, where the literature is already sparse. This work is an attempt to restore the balance at least in some small part.

The main thrust of this work is to provide the reader with a description and identification of the processes and forces that contribute to change and continuity in Qatari society. For this, a study of the history of Qatar during the past two centuries is essential, with emphasis not only on its own internal development, but also on its relationship with its closest neighbours, Bahrain and Saudi Arabia, as well as with the Ottoman Empire and Britain. It has been compiled largely from the material available at the India Office Records (Foreign and Commonwealth Office) in London together with the few existing Qatari chronicles. The former is still one of the greatest sources for the history of the entire Gulf region, although the information on Qatar is scanty compared with other places. An attempt is then made to determine the inner logic of the Qatari political and social structure and how it has evolved over the years. It will be shown how the same society that exhibited great fortitude in the face of economic and political hardship could have an equally great capacity to adapt to new levels of prosperity.

Furthermore, Qatar is viewed within the context of the entire Gulf region. Whenever possible, reference is made to a similar characteristic or incident in another part of the Gulf littoral. The pattern of Qatar's various relationships with its neighbours is also examined in order to gain a perspective of the region as a whole. Finally, the prospects for Qatar in the year 2000 will be presented as a logical continuation of past and current trends.

Notes

1. 'Qatar', *Financial Times*, 22 February 1978.
2. Ragei el Mallakh, *Qatar: Development of an Oil Economy* (London, 1979).

1 INTRODUCTION

1. Geography and Physical Characteristics

The location and geographical features of Qatar have played a predominant role in the shaping of its political and social characteristics. A narrow limestone peninsula around 22,000 square kilometres in area, Qatar juts out midway onto the Arab (western) coast of the Gulf, around 30 kilometres south of the Bahrain islands. The peninsula is largely desert with undulating rock rising out of it, making the soil generally unfit for anything but nomadic pastoralism; in fact, until the discovery of oil enabled limited agricultural activity to be financed, the only natural vegetation in Qatar, apart from a few date gardens, was coarse grass and occasional stunted brushwood. To the north, east and west, Qatar is bounded by the sea. The southern boundary, by contrast, remained undefined until the 1930s; it was closely connected with prevailing political conditions in the central and eastern part of Arabia until the delimitation of boundaries became an imperative adjunct to the acquisition of concessions by the oil companies. At the base of the eastern side of Qatar is Khawr al-Udayd, a creek that forms the boundary with the neighbouring shaykhdom of Abu Dhabi, and at its western base is Dohat al-Salwa, a bay that divides Qatar from the Hasa province of Saudi Arabia.

Qatar has generally been regarded in European literature as desolate and forbidding. Palgrave, for example, saw it as 'a miserable province' and was depressed by what he described as 'miles on miles of low barren hills, bleak and sun-scorched, with hardly a single tree to vary their dry monotonous outline'.[1] This attitude was reflected by many others, and has persisted because of the long isolation of Qatar which has only recently started to be lifted.

Placed in the context of the Arab shaykhdoms of the Gulf, however, Qatar is only strikingly different in one respect: it has never had any permanent inland settlements. All towns and villages have been coastal, with pearling, fishing and sailing the only occupations of the inhabitants. In the Trucial States, by contrast, the large inland oases — such as Buraimi (Al-Ain) in Abu Dhabi, and Dhayd in Sharjah — have provided an added dimension to the political, social and economic structure of the states in which they exist. The tribes living there have often had a powerful impact on those of the coast; the agricultural community, rudimentary though its methods might be, differs substantially from the seafaring people of the coast, providing them with necessary products they would otherwise have to import. The only Trucial State with no such oases or inland towns is Dubai. Although Dubai is much smaller than Qatar, consisting primarily of Dubai town, a strong affinity between the two places has grown up over the years. Marriage between their ruling families and a unified currency, the Qatar-Dubai riyal,[2] are but two recent examples of this.

The absence of inland settlements has made Qatar dependent commercially and politically on its neighbours. Most food has always had to be imported, together with such essential materials as wood for ships. Pearls, its main commodity until the advent of oil, were exported to Bahrain and Lingeh across the Gulf on the Persian coast where many Arabs were engaged in trade. The fact that its southern border was contiguous with the Arabian mainland made it susceptible to the political ramifications that accompanied the bedouin tribes in their inland wanderings to the various wells that dot the desert. Above all, its central location on the Arabian coast of the Gulf very often made it an outpost and a convenient place of shelter in the rather stormy political life of the Gulf states.

An examination of the map of Qatar will reveal much of its political and economic evolution during the past two hundred years. Largely because of geographic proximity, its longest and most historic links have been with Bahrain. During the second half of the eighteenth century, the Al-Khalifah, emigrants of the Utub tribe from Nejd, migrated from Kuwait and settled in the town of Zubarah, on the west coast of the peninsula. Until then, the only settled places were the villages of Huwaylah, Fuwayrat and Doha on the east coast.[3] After the founding of Zubarah, a number of villages sprang up along the west coast.

In 1783, the Utub conquered Bahrain, thus establishing the rule of Al-Khalifah which continues until today. During the next century, events in Qatar became closely tied to the affairs of Bahrain, and the shaykh of Bahrain became the accepted suzerain of Qatar. Throughout that time, the villages on the eastern and western coasts of the peninsula developed in different directions. The west coast remained linked to events in Bahrain: around 1842, for example, an exiled member of the Al-Khalifah rebuilt Zubarah, which had gone into decline, in order to launch an expedition against Bahrain. The east coast, by contrast, developed away from Bahrain.

The eastern towns and villages were practically the only inhabited parts of Qatar by the mid-nineteenth century. The largest and most important of these was Doha (often referred to as al-Bida) which grew from a tiny fishing village in the eighteenth century into a town of around 12,000 in the late nineteenth century: although there is no evidence of any population growth until the middle of the present century, it has remained the largest town of Qatar. Today it is the capital of Qatar and has a population of around 180,000. The second most important town until the contemporary age was Wakrah, 15 kilometres south-east of Doha. Other towns on the eastern coast were Ruways, almost at the tip of the promontory, Fuwayrat, Dhakhirah and Khawr Shaqiq. The latter, around 40 kilometres north of Doha, is today the second city of Qatar, known simply as Al-Khawr.

Once the tribal leaders of Qatar began to question the authority of Bahrain in the second half of the nineteenth century, the pattern was already established. There were only three towns, apart from Zubarah, on the west coast by the end of the nineteenth century: Abu Dhaluf, Hadiyah and Khawr Hassan (the latter town known as Khuwayr today). It was estimated that in 1908 the total population of these three villages did not exceed eight hundred people; by then, Zubarah was practically deserted, making the population of the west coast roughly 3 per cent of the total estimate of 27,000 in Qatar.

The location of the villages was determined by the existence of water. By and large, the settlements were made in a coastal area that was closest to a water well — usually up to four kilometres away. Until recently, the towns and villages were simple and poor, and resembled all the towns along the shores of the Gulf. Narrow and uneven winding lanes separated the houses; those of the wealthy were made of stone, the poor contenting themselves with mud. Most of the towns had a square fort with towers, the symbol of the most powerful man whose responsibility it was to protect the townspeople from marauding bedouin. The harshness of the geographic features is reinforced by the severe weather conditions: long, oppressively hot and humid summers where the temperature can reach 50°C; and short, dry, but pleasant winters. Furthermore, a strong north-west wind, the *shamal*, made sailing dangerous along the uneven coast of Qatar before the construction of modern harbours. In the last few years the geography of Qatar has changed yet again. Helped largely by the income derived from petroleum resources and the accompanying wave of imported manpower, towns and cities have mushroomed all around Qatar, east and west.

2. Population

The social structure of the population of Qatar, similar to that elsewhere in the Gulf, was made up of bedouin (*badu*) and the settled people (*hadar*), both tribally constructed. The bedouin roamed the inland regions, with their camels, sheep and goats, occasionally tending those of the settled population. They usually only entered Qatar from the Arabian mainland during the winter months, when the rainfall, although slight, permitted the growth of scrub; the rest of the time they remained in Nejd and Hasa.

As a rule, every tribe has its *dirah*, the area its members roam together as a collective body in search of grazing. The fact that a *dirah* was a well-defined place in the seemingly unending sea of sand that constitutes all desert areas, particularly those of Qatar, is an indication of the highly developed sense of geography of the different tribal groupings. They had a very sophisticated understanding of weather conditions and could generally gauge the time and distance between the desert wells. A special feature of the wells in Qatar was that, by and large, they were lined with stone in order to resist the sand. Although the bedouins' migratory habits were dominated by the landscape and the weather, their way of life was ideal for the strengthening of tribal ties.

The shaykh was the leader of the tribe, responsible for the welfare of his people. Although his position of authority could be challenged by a member of his tribe, that member would have to prove his strength and abilities if he wanted to claim the role of shaykh; otherwise, the tribe depended on the shaykh for guidance, and respected his authority. In the Trucial States, the friendship of the shaykh of a bedouin tribe, who was regarded as an independent leader, was usually sought after by the rulers of the different shaykhdoms; since he controlled a section of the hinterland, together with its people, this fact placed him in a special position of strength. Furthermore, his standing was enhanced by the competition of the neighbouring countries of Muscat and Saudi Arabia for his allegiance.

In Qatar, the situation was strikingly different. The bedouin tribes that came to graze in considerable numbers in the peninsula during the winter months were, by and large, not indigenous to the peninsula. Only one major tribe with fairly large numbers, the Bani Hajir, and another smaller and relatively unimportant tribe, the Kaban, could be regarded as belonging to Qatar proper; both tribes, however, had branches elsewhere, the former in Hasa, the latter in Bahrain. The others came from Trucial Oman and Hasa.

The significance of this for the ruler of Qatar is obvious. In Arabian society, the ultimate gauge of a ruler's authority is his ability to command the tribes who live in the land he claims; the extent of his land was thus determined by his ability to rally the tribes that roamed the area. According to desert law, a ruler's territory extended as far as he could enforce the payment of *zakat*.[4] This tax was paid by the tribes whose *dirah* the ruler claimed as his own, in return for which he ensured their protection. However, many of the tribes that came to Qatar during the winter owed allegiance to the Wahhabis. The ruler of Qatar consequently had to contend with a precarious political situation whereby he had little control over the interior, particularly when the strength of the Wahhabis culminated in the establishment of Saudi Arabia. The fact that the migratory tribes were practically transients – the winter never lasted more than three to four months – did little to bolster the authority of Qatar.

The principal bedouin tribes that migrated to Qatar from Hasa were the Murrah and the Ajman. Those that came from Trucial Oman were the Manasir; and the Naim, the other important tribe, fluctuated between Bahrain and Trucial Oman. The pattern of the migratory population of Qatar could thus be seen as almost mosaical in the power structure of the peninsula; their vicissitudes caused considerable apprehension in the coastal towns and villages, Doha being the most prominent. The Bani Hajir, for example, who were allied by religion to the Wahhabis, paid the latter *zakat*, and at the same time received gifts from the ruler of Qatar. The role of the bedouin in the political evolution of Qatar cannot be underestimated, since they could hold most of the settled places at their mercy. The Murrah were perhaps the most feared of all the tribes, with the Bani Hajir coming a close second. It is interesting to note here how the sociological observations of Ibn Khaldun regarding the encroachment of the desert on settled communities, were still reflected in the society of the Arabian peninsula four and five hundred years later.[5]

The *hadar* lived in the towns and villages where their principal activities consisted of pearl-diving and trading, fishing and sea transportation. Until very recently, when the great influx of foreigners changed the demographic characteristics of Qatar, the most populous of the sedentary tribes of the coastal districts were: the Sultan, the Mahandah, the Sudan, Al-bu-Kawarah, Hamaydat, Huwalah, Al-bu-Aynayn and the Al-bin-Ali. Table 1.1 gives an indication of the names and location of some of these tribes in 1908 and 1939. There were also a few Shiah Arabs known as Baharinah. Furthermore, by the turn of the present century, a small number of Persians had immigrated to Doha and Wakrah; by the 1930s, largely because of the new situation in Iran, almost 20 per cent of the settled population of Qatar was made up of Persians. These were in addition to the Huwalah Arabs living in Qatar; the Huwalah were Sunni Muslims who had lived on the Persian coast of the Gulf and had returned to the Arab side at a later date. Another large segment of the settled population were the negroes, descendants of the slaves who had been brought to the Gulf from East Africa during the nineteenth century. Over the years, one-third of them had been able to buy their own manumission, primarily through their work in pearling. The rest remained enslaved until the middle of the present century. Despite their obviously inferior status, the Africans gradually became integrated into Qatari society, many even assuming the names of their owners. Today they are simply considered as Qataris.

The system of government in Qatar developed along with its political evolution. Until the arrival of the Utub in 1783, no more than three tiny fishing villages existed, Huwaylah, Fuwayrat and Doha; each was dominated by the Al-Musallam; the Sudan; and the Maadhid and Al-bin-Ali tribes respectively. Although little is known of how any kind of local authority was established then, it can be assumed that the shaykh of each of these tribes was the leader of his village, and each village was autonomous. As time went by, and Qatar became a dependency of Bahrain, the peninsula was governed by a representative of the ruler of Bahrain.

All in all, therefore, almost half of the population of Qatar immediately prior to the oil era were foreigners — Baharinah, Iranians and Africans. The common experiences they shared with the local people over the years gradually welded them together, and today another, even larger and considerably more diverse, influx of foreigners has taken place.

Towards the end of the nineteenth century, the Al-Thani grew to prominence as the leading family of Qatar. As their relationship with first the Ottomans and later the British government of India developed, their position was given an added acknowledgement of authority. By the early decades of the present century, the Al-Thani were recognised as the ruling family of Qatar.

The position of the ruler was not easy. There was no rule of primogeniture in Gulf society, so that accession was rarely a smooth process. The position could be fiercely contested by up to four or five immediate relatives. The ruler therefore had to placate his family throughout the period of his rule; the fact of their birth gave them

Table 1.1: Inhabitants of Qatar: 1908 and 1939

Tribe or Community	Where Found in Qatar	Population	
		1908[a]	1939[b]
Aynayn (Al-bu-)	Wakrah	2,000	—
Ali (Al-bin-)	Doha	1,750	1,750
Amamarah	Doha and Wakrah	200	200
Arabs of Nejd	Doha and Wakrah	500	500
Baharinah	Doha and Wakrah	500	500
Baqaqalah	Doha	50	50
Dawasir	Doha	150	150
Hamaydat	Lusail and Dhaayn	250	250
Huwalah	Doha and Wakrah	2,000	2,000
Khalayfat	Wakrah	850	850
Kibisah	Khawr Hassan, Fuwayrat, Hadiyah and Sumaysmah	700	700
Kawarah (Al-bu-)	Sumaysmah, Dhaayn and Fuwayrat	2,500	2,500
Maadhid	Doha, Wakrah and Lusail	875	875
Madhahakah	Dhaayn	A few	A few
Mahandah	Khawr Shaqiq and Dhakhirah	2,500	2,500
Mananaah	Abu Dhaluf and Doha	400	400
Maqla (Al-bin-)	Wakrah	50	50
Musallam (Al-)	Doha, Fuwayrat and Wakrah	40	40
Negroes (free)	Doha and Wakrah	2,000	2,000
Negroes (slaves, but not living in their masters' houses)	Doha and Wakrah	4,000	4,000
Negroes (slaves, living with their owners)		Are reckoned in this table to the tribe in which they are owned	
Persians	Doha and Wakrah	425	5,000
Sadah	Ruways and Doha	350	350
Sudan	Doha	400	400
Sulutah	Doha	3,250	2,500
Yas (Bani) of the Al-bu-Falasah and Qubaysat sections	Doha and Wakrah	125	125

Source: a. J. G. Lorimer, *Gazeteer of the Persian Gulf, 'Oman and Central Arabia,* 5 vols. (Calcutta, 1908-15, republished by Gregg International, Westmead, UK, 1970), vol. II, p.1515.
b. L/P & S/20: C.252: Military Report and Route Book: The Arabian States of the Persian Gulf, General Staff, India, 1939, pp.92-3.

the right to challenge him, and any weakness or injustice could be seized upon to dethrone him. The members of the ruling family were always consulted before any major decision was taken, and were paid a regular stipend out of the ruler's income.

The ruler governed in a paternal fashion. He was the sole source of power, and conducted all the administration of Qatar himself. No government services or departments existed until very recently. Although he governed with absolute authority, he would often consult his *majlis* (assembly of notables) on matters of unusual importance. He was supposed to remain accessible to his people since they had recourse to no one else for their petitions and problems. He also had to reassure his people of his protection, particularly from the inland bedouins, and often paid the latter large subsidies to obtain this security. After Qatar entered into treaty relations with Britain, the ruler also had to contend with maintaining the conditions of the new agreements.

3. Socio-Economic Considerations

No understanding of the social evolution of Qatar, together with those of the other Gulf states, is possible without an awareness of the resourcefulness with which the people overcame their poverty. Qatar had an extremely scanty supply of fresh water and consequently could not rely on even a subsistence level of agriculture. The only resource was the sea. It was from the sea that the Qataris made their living, exporting their one precious commodity, the pearl.

The pearling industry was the pivotal point of the economic and social structure of Qatar. It was highly organised, functioning on a developed and familiar pattern. The boats, made by Persian and Bahraini carpenters, would usually carry around sixteen men. They would set off for the pearl banks in May, each fleet by district, and would not usually return until the end of the season, the *gaffal*, around the end of September. It is interesting to note that the captain, the *nakhoda*, was expert in finding the pearl banks, guided by the sun, stars, colours and depth of the sea.

Life aboard these boats was hard and dangerous. The division of labour was well-defined, and all members of the crew functioned according to a system that had evolved over long years of experience. The captains, divers, haulers, cooks and apprentices all lived in cramped surroundings under the blistering heat of the sun. The divers had by far the most difficult role to play, and it was for this reason that so many slaves were brought to the Gulf region. Their noses held by wooden pegs, they journeyed to the bottom of the sea with the help of ropes that were anchored down to the sea-bed, a depth of around five metres. They then had to fetch as many oysters as they could, for time was short (a maximum of one minute under water was the average) and sharks and jellyfish plentiful, to say nothing of the danger of strong currents. When the diver tugged at his rope, the response of the haulers had to be immediate in view of the dangers involved. A diver would make around fifty dives per day. Then the crew as a whole would begin cracking open the oysters, extracting the pearls, dividing them according to quality and size, and preserving the shells for mother-of-pearl. In the evening, the crews of different ships visited each other, drank coffee and exchanged news. There was a gentleman's agreement between all of them not to quarrel during the season, and feuding tribes would often anchor peacefully side by side.

The financial regulations were as well-defined as the actual fishing. Whether or not they owned their own boats, the *nakhodas* usually borrowed money from a specific kind of businessman, the *musaqqam*, at the beginning of the season to pay for the provisions to be used on board as well as to give advances to the divers. The divers in their turn were usually indebted to the *nakhodas* who charged them very high interest rates on the advances. After *gaffal*, all debts had to be paid plus interest rates. The payment was usually in instalments, and divers owing money to *nakhodas* became so indebted that they were obliged to work off their debts which, if still outstanding, were often inherited by their sons. If the *nakhoda* could not in turn repay his debt at *gaffal*, he sold his entire crop to the *musaqqam* at around 20 per cent below market price, losing the whole season's profit.

Over and above these financial regulations, the ruler levied a tax on the pearl ships, which, together with customs dues, formed the basis of his revenue. Until the Al-Thani established their authority all over Qatar, they only levied taxes in Doha and Wakrah. In both places, the tax on every *nakhoda*, hauler and diver was (Maria Theresa dollars) MT$4, and MT$2 for each apprentice, or around 7s. and 3s. 6d. respectively. In Doha, the Sudan tribe were exempt from taxes, and in 1908 it was estimated that the Al-Thani collected only MT$8,400 (£750) annually (as compared with MT$20,000 (£1,786) to MT$60,000 (£5,357) in Kuwait). It must be noted, however, that in places like the Trucial Coast, a good part of the revenue was distributed to the bedouin to protect the towns during the season. The comparative figure for Wakrah was estimated at MT$3,400 (£304). In other towns in Qatar, there was no fixed sum on pearl taxes, but the returning crew had to pay the bedouin for guarding their towns.[6]

The extent to which Qatar relied on the pearling industry for its livelihood can best be illustrated by comparing the ratio of its pearling manpower to that of the total population in Qatar with comparable figures on the Trucial Coast, Kuwait and Bahrain. It will be seen from Table 1.2 that almost half of the total population was engaged in pearling; only 18, 25 and 31 per cent of the total population of Bahrain, Kuwait and the Trucial Coast respectively were likewise engaged. Bearing in mind that 50 per cent of the population were men, the entire male population probably left the main towns for the pearling banks during the season. It is also important to note here that until 1916, when Qatar formally entered into treaty relations with Britain, it was the only place in the Arab side of the Gulf which did not receive protection from the British navy for its pearling vessels.

Table 1.2: The Pearling Industry

	Total Population	Labour Force Engaged in Pearling	Per Cent of Population in Pearling
Qatar	27,000	12,890	48
Trucial Coast	72,000	22,045	31
Kuwait	37,000	9,200	25
Bahrain	99,075	17,633	18

Source: information compiled from Lorimer, *Gazeteer*, I, pp. 2256-9.

A number of Persians and Indians came to Qatar during the nineteenth century to participate in the pearl trade. However by the early twentieth century, Qatar was unique in the Gulf in having only one resident Indian. By this time, the Al-Thani were actively engaged in the trade; and the Indians who were British subjects did not want to compete with them, particularly since Qatar had no treaty relations with Britain until 1916, and they could not claim the special privileges that they enjoyed in Bahrain and the Trucial Coast. The Persians, on the other hand, grew in number, particularly during the inter-war years as a result of the unsettled conditions in Iran together with the high taxation there.

We have already noted that Qatar had a large African population, two-thirds of whom were slaves. Most of the slaves in the Gulf had been put to work in the pearl fisheries. Almost half of the pearling population of Qatar were negroes, either slaves or former slaves; it is clear, therefore, that without this substantial addition to the population, the pearling fleet and its products would have been considerably less. Although household slaves also existed, their exact number is difficult to ascertain because they gradually became a part of the families they worked for.

Although, of course, England was heavily involved in the slave trade before that date, English courts had decided in the late eighteenth century that any slave was automatically freed the moment he set foot in England. Different regulations concerning the repression of the slave trade continued, culminating in the liberation of all slaves in British dominions a few decades later. Once Britain became actively involved in the Gulf, it made a number of agreements with the rulers of Bahrain, the Trucial States and Muscat during the nineteenth century that bound them to suppress and abstain from the slave trade, at the same time authorising the British navy to search Arab ships for slaves. These treaties curtailed the slave trade substantially, but did not suppress it entirely. It was probably because Qatar had had no relations with Britain during this time that it had such a large negro and slave population. However, when he signed a treaty with Britain in 1916, the ruler of Qatar undertook to enforce the same anti-slavery regulations as the other Trucial Coast rulers, but he and his people were allowed to retain slaves already in their possession on the condition that they treated them well.[7] The British authorities found it impossible to eliminate slavery in the Gulf, particularly when it came to domestic slaves who preferred the economic stability of a guaranteed roof over their heads, especially during the 1930s when financial hardship was at its highest. The British reserved the right, however, to issue certificates of manumission to any slave who wished to be freed; yet in the 1920s and 1930s the annual number of manumitted slaves rarely exceeded 20 or 30 for the entire Gulf region.

The pearling season determined the economic future of the Qataris until the following May. By and large, the market for their pearls was good, although, of course, the pearl merchant, the *tawwash*, never obtained the true value of the pearl, and, in descending order down to the divers, the proceeds compared to the perfection of the pearls were low. The trade was dealt a crippling blow, from which it never recovered, in the 1930s. The international economic depression of 1929, which appreciably decreased the demand for luxury items, coincided with the introduction into world markets of the Japanese cultured pearl. The combination of these two factors was a major setback for the economy of the entire Gulf region and led to a period of unprecedented hardship during which barely a handful of pearls were sold annually.

Despite the decline of the pearl industry, which in any case rarely made many of them rich, the Qataris aptly managed their few remaining resources in order to survive. The sea provided them with two other means of livelihood, fishing and sailing. Fish of all kinds were plentiful and a staple part of the Qatari diet; and the Qatari fishing fleet was around a quarter the size of its pearling fleet. Furthermore, transport ships carried goods to places like Bahrain and Lingeh.

In 1908, Lorimer estimated that there were around 1,430 camels in Qatar.[8] The camel was obviously well suited to the local environment. It produced milk, which, together with dates and fish, formed the basis of the local diet. Since few roads existed until the contemporary era, the camel was also used for local transport, to carry passengers and goods to and from various places in the peninsula. Furthermore, the camel was used to operate the wells that existed in and around all towns and villages. Qatar was one of the rare places on the Arab side of the Gulf to have a few horses, but it does not appear that they were ever exported. Sheep and goats for the settled people were tended by the bedouin, and there was a small trade exporting these to Bahrain.

It is clear from the above description of economic activities that there was little time for any luxuries. Imports were restricted to the bare necessities for the pearling fleet: wood to build boats, ropes for diving, and foodstuffs to supplement the home-grown diet. Dates were imported from Hasa, and cloth, mostly cotton bales, was imported from India, usually by way of Bahrain and Lingeh. The pace of day-to-day living was slow. Until around thirty-five years ago, there were no telephones, telegraphs or wireless communications in Qatar. Furthermore, no shipping line ever made regular calls there, communication with the outside world being entirely dependent on the local vessels of the towns and villages.

On the face of it, therefore, Qatar could easily have been overtaken by events in neighbouring or more powerful countries. The strong and complex interaction between physical geography, natural resources, Saudi, Ottoman and British interests and policies could have led to an amorphous political existence and reduced the chances for the development of a state. Yet a series of powerful men, through a purposeful and clever management of events and opportunities, successfully laid the foundations for a separate political entity. The following chapters aim to unravel these forces and to exhibit their interaction.

Notes

1. W. G. Palgrave, *Personal Narrative of a Year's Journey through Central and Eastern Arabia* (London, 1877), p. 386.

2. In May 1973, the Qatar riyal (1978 value, 3.84 = $1) replaced the Qatar-Dubai riyal in Qatar.

3. There is some fragmentary evidence that there was a settlement on the west coast, however, before Zubarah was founded; this was the village of Dawhat-al-Ruwaydah whose inhabitants migrated to Zubarah when it was founded. See J. G. Lorimer, *Gazeteer of the Persian Gulf, 'Oman and Central Arabia,* 5 vols. (Calcutta, 1908-15, republished by Gregg International, Westmead, UK, 1970), vol. II, p. 1515.

4. Permutation of the alms tax, one of the principal obligations of Islam that had its roots in the initial reluctance of the bedouin to pay it, thus becoming an enforced levy.

5. Charles Issawi, *An Arab Philosophy of History* (London, 1950).

6. Lorimer, *Gazeteer*, I, pp. 2288-9.

7. L/P & S/18: Memorandum B. 407 (P. 5301/28): Slavery in the Persian Gulf, 29 September 1928.

8. Lorimer, *Gazeteer*, vol II, p. 1533.

2 BAHRAIN AND THE AL-KHALIFAH, 1766-1820

1. Settlement of Zubarah, 1766

Qatar lies around the midway point of the Arab shores of the Gulf, in itself one of the oldest sea routes in history. It has always been most close to the Bahrain islands and to Hasa, the eastern coast of present-day Saudi Arabia. Contemporary archaeological findings confirm that the west coast of Qatar was linked with the great trading centre of Dilmun (present-day Bahrain), famous since the third millennium for its economic ties with both India and Mesopotamia. Qatar was also connected with the trade route of the famous port of Gerrha (probably the Qatif of today) in Hasa during the ninth century BC, from where the great caravan routes both across the Arabian desert and north into Mesopotamia started. But it was between the ninth and fourteenth centuries AD that the Arab coast of the Gulf reached its zenith as a great entrepôt for goods as well as a powerful strategic, communications, trade and financial centre. The Arab coast was not the only active part of the Gulf, however, the eastern or Persian coast coming into its own sometime during the classical period of Greco-Roman civilisation.

From that time to the present day, political events in the Gulf have been dominated by the rivalry between the west and east coasts, between the Arabs and the Persians. Over this long period of time, there was a considerable intermingling of the two peoples.[1] The Persians lived on the Arab coasts because of their conquest of certain areas, because they wished to partake of the rich trade, or because they needed to escape political oppression; and the Arabs had a similar experience. The same situation exists today with the result that both coastal populations contain a mixture of Arabs and Persians. Towns and cities could also claim both Arab and Persian rule. Hormuz, on the Persian side, for example, was the centre of all Gulf trade during the Middle Ages; it was ruled by Arab princes for around three centuries, after which it fell to Persian rule. The basic difference between the two is that since the modern period the Arab coastal region was never united under one ruler, while every strong Persian government was able to extend its rule to the Gulf coast.

After the successful voyage of Vasco da Gama to the Cape of Good Hope in 1498 and the subsequent entry of the Portuguese to the east, the Gulf, because of its enormous strategic importance on the rich route to India, became exposed to foreign penetration. For the next four centuries, the history of the Gulf region became inextricably linked with the political and commercial rivalries of western countries — Portugal, Holland, France and then England; to this was added the rivalry of the Ottomans from the early sixteenth century when first Baghdad and then Basra became a part of their Empire, thus making the Gulf an added concern of the Porte.

It was during the sixteenth century that the Portuguese domination of the Gulf reached its zenith. Albuquerque first took Muscat, a famous trading and communications centre, and thereby controlled most of the ports on the southern and eastern coasts of Oman. Then Hormuz fell to the Portuguese, and in 1521 Bahrain became another possession. Portugal was finally able to command the spice and silk route to India. This was not total, however, since the Venetians and Genoans continued to use the Aleppo route, and recent research has shown that the great ambition of the Portuguese was not entirely realised.[2] But the Portuguese met with two forces that were to severely threaten their position and ultimately cause their withdrawal from the region. The first of these was the Ottomans, who had already curbed Portuguese expansion in the Red Sea by defeating them at Jeddah in 1517; they then tried unsuccessfully to dislodge them from Hormuz. The second was the great Safavid ruler of Persia, Shah Abbas, whose rise to power was concurrent with his ambition to dominate Gulf waters. His first victory was in 1602 when he overtook Bahrain, and then his final ambition, to take back Hormuz, was brought about with the help of the English East India Company, with whom he made an alliance. But the Dutch and the French East India Companies were eager to offset the new foothold gained by the English, and the entire seventeenth century was dominated by the intense rivalry between the representatives of these three European companies.

In 1660, members of the Yaaribah tribe of Oman took back Muscat from the Portuguese, and in the early eighteenth century they took advantage of the internal weaknesses of Persia that had culminated in the 1722 Afghani invasion, and occupied Bahrain; they left the islands in the control of Huwalah Arabs who had migrated there from the Arabian mainland and the Persian coast. This heralded the rise to power of Oman. But the vicissitudes of Gulf politics being what they were, the fortunes of Persia that had gone into eclipse during the previous forty years began to change with the assumption to power of Nadir Shah in 1736. Determined to extend his rule to both shores of the Gulf, he built a navy; around 1753, he took Bahrain. He also conquered Muscat but was not able to hold it for long; the Persians were finally expelled by the governor of Sohar, Ahmad bin Said, who was the founder of the Al-bu-Said dynasty that rules Oman today.

Thus, by the middle of the eighteenth century, the Arab coast of Oman was governed by the Al-bu-Said, who consolidated their rule and regained for Muscat its former position as a great trade centre; it was during this time that they established their authority in East Africa which was to culminate in their domination of Zanzibar, the entrepôt of the rich trade in slaves and ivory.[3] Further north, the Qawasim of the area referred to as the Trucial Coast were also making their mark on history by armed conflicts with the European vessels that sailed Gulf waters; Bahrain was in the hands of the Persians; and Kuwait was a tiny village that had been settled since the early eighteenth century by the Utbi Arabs, Anizah of northern Arabia that were governed by a branch of the Utub, the Al-Sabah, who still govern Kuwait today. Of Qatar at this time, very little is known. It had played a minor and obscure role throughout the turmoil of the centuries, having had little to attract the various conquerors in the way of natural resources. It was sparsely inhabited by people who had taken refuge there from the neighbouring islands and mainland.

Its initial importance in the modern era began around 1760 when some members of the Utub from Kuwait migrated to Zubarah. Their principal branch there, the Al-Khalifah, was later followed to the town by another branch, the Jalahimah. With time, they developed Zubarah, and it became an important pearling and trade centre. Its commercial importance grew after Basra was taken by the Persians in 1776, when many of its inhabitants migrated south to Zubarah. Merchants, native and foreign, lived there in prosperity, no customs dues ever being levied. But the Persians regarded the rise of Zubarah as a threat, particularly after it became clear that the Imam (or spiritual leader) of Oman could be counted on as an ally of the Utub against them. Before long, hostilities between the Persians and the Utub broke out, and in 1782 the latter, together with some of the local residents of Qatar, made their first incursion into Bahrain. After a Persian retaliatory offensive against Zubarah failed, the Utub and their force tried again, in 1783 finally capturing Bahrain from the Persians.

The Al-Khalifah and most of their followers then left Zubarah and settled permanently in Bahrain where Ahmad bin Khalifah became the first member of the family to rule Bahrain, a rule that continues today. Bahrain superseded Zubarah as an important trading centre; like Zubarah, it attracted a large business community mainly because no customs duties were levied there. Equally important, perhaps, was the fact that the Bahrain pearl was found to have qualities of exceptional importance, thus adding to the commercial growth of Bahrain. For almost two centuries, however, Persia refused to accept or acknowledge the rule of the Al-Khalifah, at varied intervals disrupting the prosperity of the islands by pressing a claim for Bahrain; it was not until 1970 that the Shah of Iran finally renounced this claim.

But the Al-Khalifah's immediate concern was for the enmity it now had with the Jalahimah branch of the Utub, who refused to accept their authority in Bahrain. Having shared in the conquest of the islands, they wanted to share in their rule, and felt deprived of their rightful due. Forever aware of the wrong done to them, they left Bahrain and went back to Qatar. Rather than live in Zubarah, still a bustling trade centre that was governed by the Al-Khalifah from Bahrain, they settled in Khawr Hassan a few miles north. Within a short time, Rahmah bin Jabir, the leading member of the tribe, had established his reputation as the sworn enemy of the Al-Khalifah, and started the long process of avenging his tribe. The history of Qatar during the next fifty years revolves around the repercussions of Rahmah's career.

2. Rahmah, the Wahhabis and Oman

Four events occurred during the latter part of the eighteenth and the early part of the nineteenth centuries that were to leave a strong imprint on the Gulf region for the next two hundred years. The earliest of these was Clive's victories in India which established British dominance on the north-east coast of India, thus paving the way for further British penetration of the subcontinent; this was to lead to the growth of British interests in the Gulf as a means to preserve and protect their route to India. The second was the expansion of the Wahhabi movement[4] outside Nejd in central Arabia where it came into direct contact with the eastern coast of the Arabian peninsula. It was Abdel Aziz ibn Saud and his son Saud (1792-1814) who were largely responsible for the spread of the Wahhabi movement in the early nineteenth century. The third was the reign of one of the greatest rulers of the Sultanate of Muscat and Oman, Sayyid Said bin Sultan (1807-56). And the fourth was the rise to power of Muhammad Ali, the Albanian officer in command of Ottoman troops in Egypt, who was to establish his dynasty in Egypt. All four events were to have strong repercussions in the Gulf region, not least in Qatar itself.

It was Rahmah bin Jabir who was to set these forces in motion in Qatar. His implacable enmity with the Al-Khalifah sent him in search of new alliances that would enable him to strike at Bahrain, all the while conducting his own war against their ships. A flamboyant character, his single-mindedness made him a powerful enemy. He did not hesitate when it came to choosing or leaving allies; the only factor of importance was whether they, like him, could regard the Al-Khalifah as adversaries. His first and most important alliance was with the Wahhabis, and through them, with their allies, the Qawasim. In 1787 and 1788 the Wahhabis had made their first incursion into Qatar under Sulayman bin Ufaysan, penetrating the western coast north of Zubarah.[5] In the meantime, Rahmah, with the Qawasim of the Trucial Coast, continued seafaring activities against the Utub of Kuwait and Bahrain, also attacking Persian ships. All told, considerable losses were suffered by both the Utub and the Persians. In order to seek redress, the Persians tried to attack Khawr Hassan in 1809, but were soundly defeated, losing much in men and ships.

Rahmah's alliance with the Wahhabis continued to be strengthened, and by 1809 they were together able to subdue Zubarah and the rest of Qatar, bringing it under their joint control. Here it must be noted that in 1800, the Wahhabis had extended their influence to the Gulf when they had captured Qatif, thus bringing all of Hasa, previously governed by the Bani Khalid tribe, under their control. The same year they occupied the Buraimi oasis, the main link to both Oman and the Trucial Coast. The proximity of the Wahhabis at Zubarah and Qatif made it difficult for the Bahrainis to resist their influence for long, and by 1810 the inevitable happened; Qatif, Qatar and Bahrain were joined together under a Wahhabi governor, Abdallah bin Ufaysan. Bahrain had had a difficult decade. In 1800 and again in 1802, for a few months at a time, it had been occupied by Omani forces attracted by the wealth of the islands. In order to resist these forces, the Al-Khalifah were obliged to take refuge in a Wahhabi alliance, the result of which was the loss of their sovereignty in 1810.

The Wahhabi governorship of Bahrain infuriated the Omanis. By now, Sayyid Said bin Sultan was in power, and he could not tolerate the presence of the Wahhabis. He had, in fact, come to power by killing his pro-Saudi uncle, and until the end of his life he maintained his opposition to the new movement. It was inevitable that the Omanis and Saudis should be such implacable foes. Both places were ruled by men of considerable force; both stood to dominate the Arabian peninsula; both combined the political and the religious in their governments; and both were physically close enough to fear the territorial expansion of the other. The rise of the Saudis was also a great threat to the

Ottomans. In 1802 the former had entered Karbala, a major Shiah city, and soon after they took control of Mecca and Medina, the two most sacred cities of Islam, together with parts of Yemen. All in all, they controlled central Arabia, the Hijaz, part of Yemen and a good part of the western shores of the Gulf. In order to crush this extraordinary expansion, the Porte authorised Muhammad Ali of Egypt to recover the Hijaz, and accordingly the Egyptian force began operations in 1811. Although Medina did not fall until the next year, after which it became relatively easy to dislodge the Wahhabis from most of the Hijaz, the Egyptian landing had had powerful repercussions in the Gulf. When he realised the imminent threats to Wahhabi influence, Sayyid Said seized the opportunity to hit out against his weakened enemies. He attacked them with a strong force in Qatar, destroying Zubarah by fire.

The Wahhabis were forced to evacuate both Bahrain and Qatar, and Rahmah bin Jabir was caught unawares. He left Qatar and settled in nearby Dammam in Hasa, relentlessly resuming his seafaring activities against the Al-Khalifah. He was greatly affected by the death in 1814 of Saud ibn Abdel Aziz, after which the Wahhabi stars declined and remained thus for the rest of Rahmah's lifetime; the continued vigour of the Egyptian expedition and the absence of a forceful successor to Saud combined to keep the Wahhabi movement in abeyance. Sayyid Said had restored the Al-Khalifah to power in Bahrain, but his insistence that they be politically subordinate to him drove them to an alliance with the Wahhabis as a protection against an Omani attack. Rahmah bin Jabir could not accept this fact, and, consistent with his entire career, switched his allegiance away from the Wahhabis and to Sayyid Said. In 1816 the latter attacked Bahrain, but his ships were defeated. Undeterred, he continued to exert various forms of pressure on the Al-Khalifah until at last in 1820 they gave him their submission and promised to send him an annual tribute.

In the meantime, Rahmah bin Jabir, having become an enemy of the Wahhabis by the fact of his alliance with Sayyid Said, could no longer live in Dammam. His fort there was destroyed and only at the eleventh hour was he able to save his family and entourage in Khawr Hassan, now under Utbi and Wahhabi domination, from enforced exile in Nejd. At a loss to do more, he moved to Bushire on the Persian coast, where he continued his naval operations against the Al-Khalifah and their new allies, the Qawasim. He joined an ill-fated Persian expedition against Bahrain in the early part of 1820 only to have his ship run aground en route.

The decline of the Wahhabis continued when Muhammad Ali's son,

Ibrahim Pasha, took Dariyyah their capital, in 1818, and then moved eastwards to dominate Hasa. There Ibrahim was helped by Rahmah, who attacked the port of Qatif; he then could resettle in Dammam in order to be close to Bahrain. His harassment of the Al-Khalifah continued at a relentless pace until the British intervened; while he had never touched a British ship, his attacks on Bahrain disturbed the maritime peace that they had established in 1820. Finally, in 1824 he agreed to a peace with the Al-Khalifah, but it was not to be lasting. By now, however, Rahmah was old and blind, and his life was nearing its end. He finally died with his boots on, in a fiercely dramatic manner. Engaged in battle with the Utub in 1826, he realised he was about to be defeated; rather than surrender, he had himself and his eight-year-old son blown up on board his ship.

> Thus ended Rahmah bin Jaubir, for so many years the scourge and terror of this part of the world, and whose death was felt as a blessing in every part of the Gulf. Equally ferocious and determined in all situations, the closing scene of his existence displayed the same stern and indomitable spirit which had characterised him all his life.[6]

3. The General Treaty of Peace, 1820

The alliance of the Al-Khalifah with the Wahhabis after 1816 had brought the former face to face with the authority of the British government of Bombay. The ruler of Bahrain had become increasingly involved in the activities of the Qawasim, whose attacks on British ships were growing in number; Bahrain soon became both a place of refuge for the Qawasim and an entrepôt for their stolen goods. In 1806, the East India Company had concluded an agreement with Sultan bin Saqr of the Qawasim in which each party undertook to respect the flag and property of the other. When the Qawasim continued to attack British ships, the East India Company responded in 1819 by sending a naval force which thoroughly destroyed Ras al-Khaimah, the stronghold of the Qawasim. This crippling defeat was followed in 1820 by the General Treaty of Peace which was signed by the chiefs of the different tribes of the Trucial Coast with the East India Company. It provided for the 'cessation of plunder and piracy by land and sea' and authorised the British Residency in the Gulf to administer the terms of the treaty; it also provided for an end to the kidnapping of slaves.[7] The following month, largely because Bahrain was still being used as a place of refuge for Qawasim boats, the two co-rulers of Bahrain, Salman bin Ahmad and Abdallah bin Ahmad, agreed to a Preliminary Treaty of Peace rather than incur the wrath of British naval power. According to this treaty, they undertook to prevent the sale of stolen goods and to abstain from aiding piracy. In exchange, they became a party to the General Treaty of Peace as signed by the Qawasim.[8]

Bahrain thus came under some form of British control. From the evidence available, it would seem that the position of Qatar in the new order of the Gulf was not given much attention; it was regarded as a dependency of Bahrain, and despite the fact that there was no specific agreement with Qatar at this time, it became *de facto* subject to the 1820 treaty conditions. Although it became clear two years later that the inhabitants of the east coast of Qatar had had no knowledge of the existence of the new treaties, they were subjected to severe punishment in 1821 because of piracies committed: *Vestal*, the East India Company vessel, destroyed the town of Doha by fire, causing the migration of a large number of its inhabitants to the islands between Qatar and Abu Dhabi.[9] When the chief British representative in the Gulf, the Political Resident, Lt McLeod, visited Doha in early 1823, he found its inhabitants and their headman, Buhur bin Jubran of the Al-bu-Aynayn tribe, quite unaware of the reasons for the catastrophe inflicted on them in 1821; but he reported that they were willing to abide by treaty regulations. Lorimer, in 1908, regretted that the enforcement of Article 3 of the General Treaty of Peace, that all ships had to fly a prescribed flag to symbolise their adherence to the treaty, was not insisted on in the case of Qatar; he was convinced that 'the maintenance of the flag might have stereotyped the dependence of Qatar on Bahrain, and with it the principle of British control over Qatar.'[10] As it was, for at least half a century after the Bahrain treaty had been signed, Qatar remained a part of Bahrain as far as the British authorities in the Gulf were concerned; it was only during the 1860s that the sovereignty of Bahrain began to be questioned.

This was partly due to the fact that Qatar had no paramount leader and that the greatest overall authority there was exercised by the Al-Khalifah of Bahrain, particularly after the death of Rahmah bin Jabir. In 1828, for example, the Shaykh of Bahrain imprisoned the most important man in Doha, Muhammad bin Khamis of the Al-bu-Aynayn tribe (who had succeeded Buhur bin Jubran) for having killed a resident of Bahrain; the resulting unrest of the tribe caused the ruler of Bahrain to destroy the Al-bu-Aynayn fort in Doha and evict the tribe from that town, settling its members in the villages of Fuwayrat and Ruways.

In 1841, Doha was again subjected to bombardment by British ships. At that time, one of the most actively sought pirates of the Gulf, Jasim bin Jabir Raqraqi, had taken refuge in Doha. Despite earlier warnings to the people of Doha not to harbour him, the Political Resident realised that Raqraqi had been using Doha as his headquarters. In February 1841, therefore, a squadron went to the town to punish the headman, Salimayn bin Nasir of the Sudan tribe. He was told to produce a fine as well as Raqraqi's ship, failing which the British guns would start to fire. A few warning shots obtained the desired result. Salimayn came forward with the fine for which he could not pay entirely in cash. He offered, amongst other items, 42 silver bracelets, one sword, one silver hair ornament, four pairs (gold) earrings, two daggers, nine bead necklaces and two silver ear-rings to supplement the money available.[11] He also handed in Raqraqi's vessel which was then publicly burned.

Qatar thus had a rather nebulous and undefined position whereby it was considered a part of Bahrain, and, through this relationship with Bahrain, it was tied to Britain and any other country or party with whom the Al-Khalifah were allied. For the half-century following the 1820 treaty, Qatar was unable to extricate itself fully from this stand. But the repercussions of its relationship with Bahrain ultimately led to the rise of a family that was to challenge the authority of the Al-Khalifah.

Notes

1. The Huwalah Arabs are an example of this. Originally Arabs, they moved to the Persian coast at different points in history, but retained their Sunni identity. At a later point, they returned to the Arab coast.

2. John Francis Guilmartin Jr, *Gunpowder and Galleys: Changing Technology and Mediterranean Warfare at Sea in the Sixteenth Century* (London, 1974).

3. See C. S. Nicholls, *The Swahili Coast* (London, 1971) for an extensive description of Omani shipping during this period.

4. Named after the founder, Muhammad bin Abd al-Wahhab. The basic ideology of this puritanical movement was to affect a return to the original principles of Islam. Their main theological tenet was the oneness or unity of God, hence the name *Muwwahidin*. In 1744, Muhammad became allied to Muhammad ibn Saud of the House of Saud in Dariyyah in Nejd, who undertook to help in the reforms. This alliance remains the basis of the Kingdom of Saudi Arabia today.

5. ARAMCO, *Oman and the Southern Shore of the Persian Gulf* (Cairo, 1952), p.212.

6. V/23/217, Bombay Selections, vol. 24, Lt S. Hennell, 'Sketch of the Proceedings (from 1809 to 1818) of Rahmah bin Jaubir, Chief of Khor Hassan', p. 528.

7. See C. U. Aitchison, *A Collection of Treaties, Engagements and Sanads relating to India and Neighbouring Countries* (Delhi, 1933), vol XI, pp. 245-9.

8. Ibid., pp. 233-4.

9. J. G. Lorimer, *Gazeteer of the Persian Gulf, 'Oman and Central Arabia,* 5 vols. (Calcutta, 1908-15, republished by Gregg International, Westmead, UK, 1970), vol. I, p. 793. Although no mention of this attack is to be found in the Bombay Proceedings, it is referred to in C. R. Low, *A History of the Indian Navy, 1615-1863* (London, 1877), vol. 1, p. 385. Here, however, it is claimed that ships off Doha were burned, rather than Doha itself.

10. Lorimer, *Gazeteer*, vol. I, p. 794.

11. L/P & S/5/393: Enclosure to Bombay Secret Letter 29 of 26 April 1841. G. B. Brucks to Capt. S. Hennell (Political Resident, henceforth Pol. Res.), 23 March 1841. See also J. B. Kelly, *Britain and the Persian Gulf, 1795-1880* (Oxford, 1968), pp. 364-5.

TRANSITION TO AUTONOMY, 1820-1913

1. Rebellion Against Bahrain: Isa bin Turayf

During the first half of the nineteenth century, the political evolution of Qatar became strongly linked to events in Hasa and Bahrain. This was largely due to the absence of any effective leadership from within Qatar itself and the special position held there by Bahrain. But the Al-Khalifah exercised only a relatively loose form of control over Qatar. During the years after the 1820 treaties that had placed most of the coastal areas from Bahrain to Ras al-Khaimah under strict British surveillance, Qatar became an outpost for the different absconding elements in the region. Around 1818, for example, Muhammad bin Shakhbut, ruler of Abu Dhabi, was deposed by his brother Tahnun; he then went to live in Doha from where, a few years later, he was to lead an unsuccessful expedition to regain his position. After his defeat, he returned to live in the town of Huwaylah in Qatar. In 1836, the first in a series of migrations of the Qubaysat, a branch of the Bani Yas (the principal tribe of Abu Dhabi, a member of which has always been the ruler) to Khawr al-Udayd took place; they left in order to escape paying their share of the compensation money that the ruler of Abu Dhabi had been forced to pay the British as a result of piracy. Their stay in Khawr al-Udayd was marked by the continuance of piracy under the leadership of Jasim bin Jabir Raqraqi and, apparently, with the help of the inhabitants of eastern Qatar. So in 1836 a British naval force went to Doha, Wakrah and Udayd 'to remind the people of Qatar of their responsibilities'.[1] The leaders of these three towns, Salimayn bin Nasir, Ali bin Nasir of the Sudan tribe and Khadim bin Naman respectively, promised to curtail the pirates or face the consequences. The shelling of Doha in 1841 (see Chapter 2) was the direct result of this agreement.

But not all involvements with neighbours were detrimental. During the 1840s Qatar became strongly linked to the civil disturbances in Bahrain, the repercussions of which were to have far-reaching consequences. Khalifah bin Muhammad, the first ruler of Bahrain, was succeeded by his son Ahmad, who died around 1796. His two sons, Salman and Abdallah, became co-rulers of the islands, an agent of the duumvirate having signed the General Treaty of 1820 (see Table 3.1). When Salman died, his son Khalifah became co-ruler with Abdallah;

when Khalifah died, it seemed natural for his son Muhammad bin Khalifah, the great-nephew of Abdallah, to continue in the tradition established by his father and grandfather. By this time, Abdallah, an old and tenacious man, had made himself thoroughly unpopular with his sons and most of his people, with the result that a widespread exodus from Bahrain began to take place. When his animosity towards Muhammad bin Khalifah became uncontrolled in 1840, the latter went to Qatar, where his popularity and authority were soon established, a direct consequence of the suffering inflicted by Abdallah on the inhabitants. In 1835, the two main tribes of the town of Huwaylah, the Al-bin-Ali and the Al-bu-Aynayn, had rebelled against Abdallah, helped by the Wahhabis and rebellious sons of Abdallah.[2] Although a tenuous peace was established by the son of Sayyid Said of Muscat, it was soon to be broken when Abdallah incited the Al-bu-Kawarah tribe of Qatar to attack Huwaylah; during the attack, a relative of Isa bin Turayf of the Al-bin-Ali, headman of the town, and brother-in-law of Abdallah, was killed. The old ruler of Bahrain staunchly refused to make any kind of reparation. Isa, unwilling to continue to live at Abdallah's mercy, led a considerable number of the Al-bin-Ali and Al-bu-Aynayn out of Qatar and into Abu Dhabi.

As the contest for the position of ruler of Bahrain continued, Qatar alternated as a base for the two opposing members of the Al-Khalifah, each man in turn making Khawr Hassan as his headquarters in the peninsula while his rival was in Bahrain. Abdallah did not last long in Khawr Hassan, however, and rather than face a hostile population, he decided to reoccupy Zubarah, by now a deserted town. He was stopped by Muhammad bin Khalifah, who was clearly in control of Qatar. Muhammad also gained control of Bahrain. In 1843, he set off for Bahrain, and with the help of Isa bin Turayf and Bishr bin Rahmah, son of Rahmah bin Jabir, he was able to obtain acknowledgement as sole ruler of the islands. Once his ally had assumed power in Bahrain, Isa returned to Doha. Before long he assumed the position of headman of the town from Salimayn bin Nasir of the Sudan tribe who had become prominent after the exodus of the Al-bin-Ali.

Abdallah bin Ahmad, however, refused to admit defeat. He established himself in nearby Dammam, which was now once more under Wahhabi rule. In 1840, all the forces of Muhammad Ali had returned to Egypt, after which Faysal bin Turki became the acclaimed Wahhabi leader. His father, Turki bin Abdullah, a cousin of the great Saud, had started the revival of Wahhabi power. but he was assassinated in 1834 and Faysal was taken prisoner to Cairo. Faysal ultimately came home from exile and for the next twenty years ruled with great strength and wisdom. While at first he offered to help Abdallah bin Ahmad, the intractability of the old man irritated him, and he soon drove him out, but not before Abdallah had made an unsuccessful attempt to destroy Isa bin Turayf at Doha.

Isa's interactions with the dynastic disturbances in Bahrain reveal that he did not regard either Muhammad or Abdallah as an ally, despite the fact that the latter was his brother-in-law; his main interest was to weaken the hold that Bahrain had over Qatar. Around 1843, for example, he approached the regent of Muscat and suggested that the latter seize the chance to conquer Bahrain, weakened by the rivalry between Muhammad and Abdallah, and that he would help him in this. The idea

Table 3.1: The Al-Khalifah of Bahrain

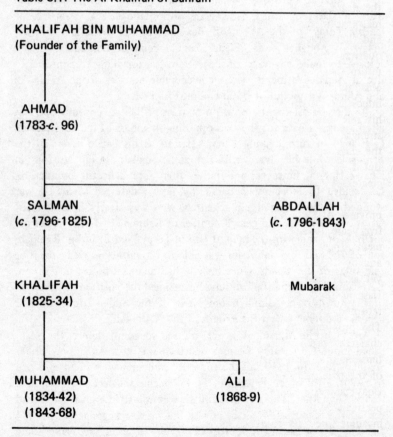

KHALIFAH BIN MUHAMMAD
(Founder of the Family)

AHMAD
(1783-c. 96)

SALMAN   ABDALLAH
(c. 1796-1825)   (c. 1796-1843)

KHALIFAH   Mubarak
(1825-34)

MUHAMMAD   ALI
(1834-42)   (1868-9)
(1843-68)

came to nothing, but within a few years Isa had become the enemy of Muhammad, the more powerful of the two claimants, openly declaring his friendship for Abdallah. He sealed his fate by fighting on the latter's side in the final and decisive battle between the two members of the Al-Khalifah in Qatar during the summer of 1847;[3] Abdallah was severely defeated and Isa killed. Although there is no evidence that Isa had sought to obtain an autonomous position for the whole of Qatar, his active attempts to weaken the Al-Khalifah hold on Doha became a landmark in the history of Qatar. The very fact that he had opposed a member of the Bahrain ruling family was to pave the way for other such actions in the future.

2. The Wahhabi Challenge to Bahrain

With the main local challenge to his authority in Qatar removed with the death of Isa bin Turayf, Muhammad bin Khalifah re-established his position there, first attacking Doha and forcing the Al-bin-Ali out and then appointing his brother Ali as his *wali* (deputy) with head-quarters in the fort of Doha. He then persuaded the Al-bin-Ali to return to Doha. It was at this time that Muhammad bin Thani of the Maadhid tribe left Fuwayrat and settled in Doha, a move of great importance to subsequent events in Qatar. Throughout the period of his rule, Muhammad bin Khalifah had to contend with the growing strength of the Wahhabis under Faysal bin Turki, to say nothing of the claim to Bahrain by both the Persian and Ottoman governments. But it was the re-establishment of the Wahhabis in Hasa that posed the greatest threat to Muhammad as ruler of both Bahrain and Qatar.

After the Egyptian occupation that lasted from 1818 to 1819, the province of Hasa reverted to the rule of the Bani Khalid for around five years. It ended when Turki bin Abdallah gave the Wahhabi move-ment a new lease on life. The Wahhabi influence began to grow again and by 1830 they were in control of Hasa once more, only to lose it yet again to the Egyptians in 1838. The Egyptian forces evacuated Hasa in 1840, after which the inevitable happened and the Wahhabis returned. By 1843, Faysal bin Turki was in full control of the province. The proximity of Hasa and Bahrain, coupled with the geographical characteristics of their location, have combined to produce the unusual tensions that have persisted between the two places until the early part of the twentieth century. In Hasa, for example, the coastal town of Uqayr and the island of Tarut are a mere 40 and 55 kilometres res-pectively away from Bahrain, ideal locations from which to launch an invading force. By contrast, the central position of the Bahrain islands along the coast of Hasa gives Bahrain a clear advantage in maritime superiority, the best example of which has been its ability to blockade Hasa ports. It was the position of Qatar, however, that could often give the successive rulers of Hasa the edge over Bahrain. For while Bahrain had to use great force to establish its rule over Qatar, it had little ability to control events in Hasa whose contiguous position with Qatar posed a constant threat to Bahrain's sovereignty. It stood to reason, therefore, that an alliance between the rulers of Hasa and Bahrain would prove highly detrimental to Qatar, depriving it of its natural leverage. In early 1840, for example, when the Egyptians, allied now with the Al-Khalifah, were still in Hasa, they were about to send a punitive expedition to Qatar because of the refusal of the Naim tribe under Jabir bin Nasir to pay *zakat*; although the assassination of a governor of Hasa (for reasons unconnected with the Naim) prevented the expedition from getting off the ground, the incident served to emphasise the vulnerability of Qatar in the face of a united front in Hasa and Bahrain.

We have already noted that Faysal bin Turki seemed willing at first to back the ex-ruler of Bahrain, Abdallah bin Ahmad, against Muhammad bin Khalifah. When the Wahhabi Amir drove Abdallah out, however, Muhammad promised to pay the Wahhabis *zakat* as compensation. For the next fifteen years the relationship between Turki and Muhammad fluctuated greatly, fierce outbreaks, blockading of Hasa ports and threats of Wahhabi invasions becoming interspersed with tenuous peace agreements. In 1850, there was a renewal of tension, and Faysal bin Turki this time reacted with determination by making his way to Qatar. While his brother Ali hurriedly returned to Bahrain from Doha, Muhammad promised to pay Faysal all the arrears in tribute that he owed, worried about the consequences of the expedition. He realised that Faysal could easily wrest control of Qatar from him, thus having an excellent base from which to launch an expedition to Bahrain. Faysal may have also been interested in establishing a port on Khawr-al-Udayd in order to obviate the disadvantages of any future Bahraini blockades on Wahhabi ports.[4] As it was, Faysal was undeterred by the offer of money made to him and proceeded in person to Qatar. With Ali away, the people of Doha, Wakrah and Fuwayrat all declared their allegiance to Faysal, who then turned his attention to Bahrain.[5]

At this point, the Political Resident sent the entire Persian Gulf squadron to Bahrain in order to protect it from Wahhabi attack. This *deus-ex-machina*,[6] of course, saved Muhammad bin Khalifah from Faysal, and a peace between the belligerents was agreed on soon after.

Ali was restored to his former position in Doha and Muhammad promised to pay the arrears in tribute to Faysal. But the peace was short-lived, Muhammad openly refusing to pay *zakat*; apparently he had also prevailed on certain people in Qatar to oppress Wahhabi subjects in Qatar by murdering them and seizing their property.[7] So preparations began for a Wahhabi attack on Bahrain. It would have succeeded except that, once again, the British squadron intervened and prevented any battle at sea. Subsequently, in 1861, Bahrain signed an agreement with the British government whereby the former agreed to the cessation of all maritime warfare in exchange for British protection from attack by sea.[8] In this agreement, as in that of 1820, Qatar was not named specifically but Bahrain's 'dependencies' were referred to: it is useful here to note that in subsequent agreements, the next one being in 1880, Bahrain's 'dependencies' were no longer mentioned.

3. The 1867 Attack on Qatar

Muhammad bin Khalifah's wings had been sharply clipped by the 1861 agreement. But he remained unchanged, and after 1865, when Faysal died, he refused to continue the *zakat* payments that were generally acknowledged to have been a security for Al-Khalifah rule in Qatar. The authority of Bahrain in Qatar had continued to be administered by a *wali*, a member of the Al-Khalifah, with headquarters in Doha. By 1867, relations between Ahmad bin Muhammad, the *wali*, who was married to the daughter of a Doha notable, Muhammad bin Thani, and the people of Qatar had become so strained that Muhammad bin Khalifah realised he would have to use force in order to maintain his position in Qatar; he was also concerned about the continued pro-Wahhabi sentiments of the people of Qatar and wanted to inflict a severe punishment on them.

The direct causes for the resulting state of events remain somewhat confused. One version has it that the *wali*, cousin of Muhammad bin Khalifah, deported a bedouin from Qatar,[9] another that he deported the headman of Wakrah,[10] and yet another that he imprisoned the headman of the Naim, Ali bin Thamir, for having protested against the injustices of the *wali* to members of his tribe in Wakrah.[11] The consequent discontent in Qatar was so strong that the *wali* was forced to leave eastern Qatar, feeling safer in Khawr Hassan, on the west coast. Once again, there is more than one version of the sequel to this. The first is that when Muhammad sent an emissary to enquire into the affair, the unfortunate man was imprisoned by the rebellious Qataris.[12] The second has it that Muhammad bin Khalifah, in an apparent effort to regulate his administration in Qatar, sent for Qasim bin Muhammad, a member of the Al-Thani family of Doha; when Qasim arrived in Bahrain, he was imprisoned.[13]

What is certain, however, is that Muhammad bin Khalifah, disregarding his recent commitment to desist from maritime warfare, began preparations for a large and powerful punitive expedition to Qatar. He was joined by Shaykh Zayid bin Khalifah of Abu Dhabi who seized the opportunity to attack the Qataris whom he regarded as allies of the Wahhabis; he sent an estimated force of 2,000 men and 70 boats. The Bahrain force, commanded by Muhammad's brother Ali, consisted of 700 men and 24 boats. The combined attack in October 1867 was devastating. Doha and Wakrah were thoroughly sacked and looted, their inhabitants only escaping death by scattering in all directions, and around 40 Qatari ships were seized. The total damage was estimated to have been equivalent to around £50,000.[14]

Although the Wahhabis made strong protests and harassed a number of Bahrainis, the people of Qatar received no other tangible help. They fought back, however. They courageously mustered their few remaining resources and set sail for Bahrain. A grim battle followed in which hundreds were killed. But no clear victory ensued, and the situation remained highly tense. Almost a year after the combined expedition had taken place, Col. Lewis Pelly, the Political Resident in the Persian Gulf, arrived in Bahrain. He was fully aware of the importance of his mission, for the attack had constituted a flagrant disregard of treaty conditions, and Britain stood to lose its position as keeper of the maritime peace in Gulf waters.

In order to make an example of him, he decided to remove Muhammad and place his brother Ali in the position of ruler. He then proceeded to obtain Ali's signature to an agreement in September 1868 whereby the new ruler undertook to pay a large fine for the violation of the 1861 agreement: around 20 per cent of the money was to go towards compensation for the people of Qatar.[15] Having settled the Bahraini side of the dispute, Pelly then sailed to Wakrah. There he met with Shaykh Muhammad bin Thani who acted as a representative for the people of Qatar. The meeting was historic, for its outcome was a written agreement that was signed by Muhammad on 12 September 1868. In it, Muhammad promised to return to Doha, which he had left after the attack; he promised to desist from maritime warfare, and not to ally himself with Muhammad bin Khalifah; and he undertook to refer to the Resident any disagreements arising from the payment of tribute to the rulers of Bahrain.[16] Pelly also drew up an agreement between Muhammad and the Shaykh of Bahrain, regulating the matter of the tribute to be paid by Qatar to Bahrain. This was listed and divided as shown in Table 3.2.

Table 3.2: Qatari Tributes to Bahrain

Krans	Tribe Paying Tribute
1,700	Mahandah tribe
1,500	Al-bu-Aynayn and Naim
500	Al-bu-Kawarah
500	Keleb
1,500	Sudan
2,500	Muhammad bin Thani (for Maadhid and Musallam tribes)
800	Amamarah
Total 9,000	

Source: C. U. Aitchison, *A Collection of Treaties, Engagements and Sanads Relating to India and Neighbouring Countries* (Delhi, 1933), vol XI, p. 193. (The sum of 9000 krans was roughly equivalent to £40).

And we, the said Cheifs, understanding that the Bahrein Chief claims from us a total of 15,000 Krans per annum in lieu of 9,000 as above set forth, we do hereby agree to pay any extra sums not aggregating a total larger than 15,000, which the Resident after judicial investigation may decree.[17]

The first step in the long road to the ultimate independence of Qatar was thus taken. The fact that the Political Resident, the foremost British representative in the Gulf, had entered into negotiations with Muhammad bin Thani gave the latter a special status that was not dissimilar to that granted to the rulers of the various Trucial States. Not only did it give him some form of recognition which he had not known hitherto; it also gave him a new dimension of power, one that was to become increasingly stratified with time because of the responsibility of his treaty conditions. That the negotiations for the agreement had taken place with such an eminent representative of the British government made it even more impressive an event. The people of Qatar were aware of the significance of the occasion, particularly as they well knew the power of the British navy that controlled their Gulf waters. Pelly underlined the new status of Muhammad bin Thani when informing the Qatari people of the agreement in a declaration made on 13 September 1868: 'It is therefore expected that all the Shaikhs and tribes of Guttar should not molest him or his tribesmen.'[18]

The beginning of the decline of the Al-Khalifah in Qatar had set in. After that, the only exercise of its suzerainty was the annual tribute paid by the Al-Thani. The Al-Thani belong to the Al-Maadhid tribe, whose founder was Maadhid bin Musharraf, one time governor of the great Jabrin oasis in central Arabia.[19] The family also claim descent from the Bani Tamim tribe of central Arabia.[20] Generally, the Maadhid are regarded as being a branch of the Al-bin-Ali, although the Al-Thani themselves repudiate any such connection. In any case, both the Maadhid and the Al-bin-Ali were settled in Fuwayrat when the Utub first arrived in Zubarah, and we have already noted that Muhammad bin Thani moved to Doha after the death of Isa bin Turayf.

Although little more is known of the rise to prominence of the Al-Thani in Qatar, it is clear that their representative had replaced the position left vacant by the death of Isa bin Turayf. Muhammad bin Thani had obviously attained a fairly well established position before 1868, particularly as he had been responsible for the annual collection of tribute in the peninsula. The impetus given the status of the Al-Thani as the leading tribe of Qatar by the Political Resident in 1868 was strengthened and reinforced when, in 1871, the Ottomans arrived in Doha following their occupation of Hasa.

Notes

1. J. G. Lorimer, *Gazeteer of the Persian Gulf, 'Oman and Central Arabia*, 5 vols. (Calcutta, 1908-15, republished by Gregg International, Westmead, UK, 1970), vol. I, p. 797. Also see V/23/217, Bombay Selections, vol. 24, 'Historical Sketch of the Beniyas Tribe of Arabs', Lt A. B. Kemball, 1832-43, pp. 478-80.

2. L/P & S/5/375: Enclosure to Bombay Secret Letter 67 of 18 May 1839. Summary by J. P. Willoughby (Secretary to Government, henceforth Sec. to Govt) of the dispute between Abdallah bin Ahmad and Isa bin Turayf, 25 February 1839.

3. The place of battle seems to be confused. Lorimer, *Gazeteer*, vol. I, p. 800, claims it was in Fuwayrat. M. S. Al-Shaybani, *Imarat Qatar al-Arabiyyah* (Beirut, 1962), pp. 56-7, claims it to be Umm al-Sawwiyah (Swaiyah today), near Khawr Shaqiq. So also does Mahmud Bahjat Sinan, *Tarikh Qatar al-Am* (Baghdad, 1966), pp. 65-6.

4. R. Bayley Winder, *Saudi Arabia in the Nineteenth Century* (New York, 1965), p. 186.

5. Reference must be made here to one version of Faysal's expedition. The people of Qatar, under Muhammad bin Thani, were determined to oppose the Wahhabis, but the Naim tribe persuaded them that they could only stand to lose in the face of the powerful army of Faysal. Al-Shaybani, *Imarat Qatar*, pp. 61-2.

6. Bayley Winder, *Saudi Arabia*, p. 187.

7. L/P & S/5/504: Enclosure to Bombay Secret Letter 13 of 27 March 1860, Faysal to F. Jones (Pol. Res.), 7 Rabi II 1276/3 November 1859.

8. C. U. Aitchison, *A Collection of Treaties, Engagements and Sanads Relating to India and Neighbouring Countries* (Delhi, 1933), vol. XI, pp. 234-6.

9. ARAMCO, *Oman and the Southern Shore of the Persian Gulf* (Cairo, 1952), p. 217.

10. Lorimer, *Gazeteer*, vol. I, p. 892, and Aitchison, *Collection of Treaties*, vol. XI, p. 192.

11. Al-Shaybani, *Imarat Qatar*, pp. 76-7.

12. J. B. Kelly, *Britain and the Persian Gulf, 1795-1880* (Oxford, 1968), p. 673.

13. Lorimer, *Gazeteer*, vol. I, p. 893; Al-Shaybani, *Imarat Qatar*, pp. 80-1.

14. L/P & S/20: C. 241, J. A. Saldana, 'A Precis of Bahrein Affairs, 1854-1904', p. 14.

15. Aitchison, *Collection of Treaties*, vol. XI, p. 193.

16. Ibid., p. 255. See Appendix II.

17. Ibid.

18. L/P & S/5/261: Appendix 8 (to Enclosure 276) in Govt of India Foreign Letter 187 of 24 October 1868 (f 912).

19. Lorimer, *Gazeteer*, vol. I, Part 3, 'Table of the Ruling Al-Thani (Ma'adhid) Family of Dohah in Qatar'.

20. ARAMCO, *Oman*, p. 204.

4 THE SEEDS OF INDEPENDENCE, 1872-1916

1. The Ottoman Period, 1872-1913

After the death of Faysal bin Turki in 1865 the decline of the second Wahhabi state set in. The intense rivalry of his two eldest sons, Abdallah and Saud, weakened the structure that Faysal had built up so carefully, and within twenty years the Wahhabi movement went into eclipse once again. Almost concurrently, the Ottomans began to take a renewed interest in the Arabian peninsula, particularly after the opening of the Suez Canal in 1866. With the Hijaz already under their control, they took Asir on the Red Sea in 1871 and the same year, under the vigorous leadership of Midhat Pasha, the *vali* of Baghdad, they occupied Hasa. Their power thus extended from the western to the eastern coast of Arabia. Within a few years, an ally of theirs, Ibn Rashid of Jabal Shammar, was able to control the central and northern parts of the peninsula. All former Wahhabi possessions had changed hands.

A few months after the Ottoman occupation of Hasa, and following a deputation to Qatar, Qasim bin Muhammad Al-Thani, son of Muhammad bin Thani, accepted the Turkish flag in Qatar. Although his father was strongly opposed to this move, Qasim's action was clearly based on pragmatic considerations: the decline of the Wahhabis in Hasa had left the people of Qatar without any protection from attacks by Bahrain, the memory of the 1867 expedition still being very vivid; and the Ottoman presence in Hasa was a reality that Qatar would obviously have to contend with. For the next forty years, Qasim (sometimes referred to as Jasim) bin Muhammad had to balance the power of the Ottomans against the growing British fears of Ottoman encroachment on their interests in the Gulf, all the while staving off Bahraini attempts to reassert its sovereignty over Qatar. Although the results sometimes left Qasim in a precarious and vulnerable position, his tenacity ultimately brought rewards to Qatar and the Al-Thani.

Qasim's quiet acceptance of the Ottoman presence in Doha, manifested by the landing of 100 troops and field guns early in 1872, quickly turned into resentment. Although his personal position as the most important local personage was not seriously threatened, he began to chafe at obvious interference in Qatar's internal affairs: the Ottoman representative in Doha, for example, was also the *qadi* (judge) of that place. Furthermore, Qatar was made to pay tribute to the Ottomans that exceeded all former sums to Bahrain, and by 1875 Qasim confided to the British representatives that he would gladly see the Ottomans leave Qatar.

On the face of it, the Ottoman presence was not all detrimental to Qasim. In 1876, he was appointed *Qaim Maqam*[1] of Qatar and three years later he was formally made the governor of Doha town. These appointments gave him a certain prestige, although in 1881 he admitted to the Political Resident that his authority did not in fact extend beyond the towns of Doha and Wakrah.[2] This particular statement could have been made to avoid responsibility for reported cases of piracy in Qatar that the British representative was investigating, for there is no doubt that it was during the Ottoman period that Qasim extended the authority of the Al-Thani throughout the peninsula of Qatar. Three factors combined to enable this to take place. The first and most important of these was the complexity of Anglo-Ottoman relations. While the British Government never officially accepted the Porte's claim of sovereignty over Qatar, it avoided any possibility of jeopardising its delicate relations with the Ottomans at a time when British policy was to maintain the territorial integrity of the Ottoman Empire in order to preserve the balance of power in Europe. The 'vexed question' of Qatar, as it was referred to by Foreign Office officials, conflicted with another, equally important, aspect of British policy: the maintenance of the Gulf as a British lake which provided a vital link in the route to India. This clash of interests was reflected in the opposing attitudes towards Qatar of the Foreign Office in London and the Government of India in Delhi.[3] The resulting situation was a curiously nebulous attitude on the part of British officials: while never actually accepting the *de jure* rule of the Porte in Qatar, they tacitly acknowledged the *de facto* situation, consequently steering clear of any embarrassing confrontation, an attitude echoed by the Ottomans who repeatedly claimed sovereignty over both Bahrain and Qatar.

The second factor was the personality and character of Qasim himself. A headstrong, sometimes rash man, he also displayed great tenacity and courage. While it is doubtful that he was aware of the many aspects of Anglo-Ottoman relations, he seemed to know intuitively the value of setting off the two powers against each other. His actions often had him walking a tightrope, but he finally emerged in a far more powerful position than the one he had inherited from his father.

The third factor was the numerous claims made by the Al-Khalifah for sovereignty over Zubarah. These claims led to armed clashes in which Britain and the Porte became involved. Both powers, however, sought to avoid the very real dangers of direct confrontation by reaching compromises. The repercussions of the Zubarah problem resulted in the polarisation of tribal loyalties upon which the Al-Thani began to rely; they also set a precedent for the Zubarah disputes of the twentieth century, the outcome of which was to be favourable to the Al-Thani. The crises of the Ottoman period were to bring a final halt to the Bahraini claims over Qatar; never again was the authority of the Al-Thani in Qatar to be seriously questioned by the Al-Khalifah.

The first claim to Zubarah during the Ottoman period was made in 1872 by Isa bin Ali, ruler of Bahrain after the death of his father in 1869.[4] His claim to Zubarah was based on the allegiance to Bahrain of the Naim tribe who usually spent the months of the summer pearling season there. One of Ali's strongest motives regarding sovereignty over Zubarah was the desire to check the intrigues of Nasir bin Mubarak, a pretender to the position of ruler of Bahrain; Isa wanted to re-establish a garrison at the town for that explicit purpose. Isa himself had come to power in 1869 when his father Ali bin Khalifah had been killed in battle against the combined forces of his own brother Muhammad, the former ruler, and Nasir bin Mubarak, grandson of Abdallah bin Ahmad (see Table 4.1). The Political Resident foresaw the possibility of Ottoman entanglement in the Zubarah issue and advised Isa to remain neutral. Isa accepted the advice but continued to regard Zubarah as a part of Bahrain, always afraid that it would be used as a base from which to launch an expedition against him.

In 1874, his fears were realised when the allies of Nasir bin Mubarak, together with a force of Bani Hajir tribesmen, collected in Zubarah in an attempt to cross into Bahrain. British ships of the Bombay Marine prevented the invasion, so the force attacked the Naim in Zubarah instead, only to be defeated. This was the first of many attempts by the British Government to neutralise the situation in Zubarah. While never encouraging the ruler of Bahrain to consider any part of Qatar as his because of the consequences that Britain might have to face with the Porte, the Political Resident also sought to prevent the use of Zubarah as a launching place for a naval expedition against Bahrain.

Although Qasim bin Muhammad might not have regarded Zubarah as part of his territory in 1871, the consequent clashes over that place resulted in the recognition of the sovereignty of the Al-Thani. In 1878, for example, together with Nasir bin Mubarak and force of 2,000 men, he sacked and destroyed Zubarah to punish the Naim for an act of piracy, and the Political Resident refused the request of Isa of Bahrain to help the Naim, many of whom had lost their homes in the fighting.

Table 4.1: The Al-Khalifah

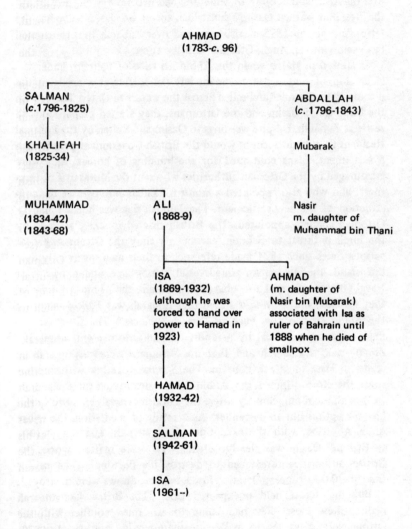

```
                          AHMAD
                         (1783-c. 96)

SALMAN                                      ABDALLAH
(c.1796-1825)                               (c. 1796-1843)

KHALIFAH                                    Mubarak
(1825-34)

MUHAMMAD           ALI                      Nasir
(1834-42)          (1868-9)                 m. daughter of
(1843-68)                                   Muhammad bin Thani

                 ISA                AHMAD
                 (1869-1932)        (m. daughter of
                 (although he was   Nasir bin Mubarak)
                 forced to hand over associated with Isa as
                 power to Hamad in  ruler of Bahrain until
                 1923)              1888 when he died of
                                    smallpox

                 HAMAD
                 (1932-42)

                 SALMAN
                 (1942-61)

                 ISA
                 (1961--)
```

Although Zubarah as a town ceased to exist after this attack, its strategic position was still important. During the 1880s, Qasim began to plan the building of an establishment in Zubarah in order to score a victory over the Al-Khalifah. By 1888, when this had become a strong possibility, the Resident warned Qasim against such an act. So Qasim turned to the Ottomans, and in 1895 a crisis occurred over Zubarah that threatened to develop into an Anglo-Ottoman conflagration.

It started in March when the Al-bin-Ali tribe of Bahrain, under the leadership of Sultan bin Salamah, left the islands as a result of the dispute with the ruler and sailed across the waters to Qatar. There, with the blessings of Qasim and the Ottomans, they started preparations to settle at Zubarah. Despite warnings to Qasim and Sultan by the Political Resident that on no account would the British Government permit such a settlement, plans continued for the building of homes; they were encouraged by the Ottoman authorities who sent the Mutasarrif of Hasa there, and who also appointed a *mudir* for Zubarah to oversee the construction of the new settlement. The Turkish flag was hoisted and six Ottoman soldiers appointed. The British reacted quickly, alarmed by the implicit threat to Bahrain, particularly since the Ottomans had at various times since 1871 made reference to their own sovereignty over the islands themselves. An armed vessel, the *Sphinx*, under the Senior Naval Officer, was sent to Zubarah to persuade the Al-bin-Ali to leave; they refused, and the *mudir* stated that Zubarah was Turkish and that the Al-bin-Ali had now become Turkish subjects.[5] The situation was made even more critical by a report that an Ottoman gun vessel, the *Zuhaf*, was at Zubarah and that the Ottomans were getting a force ready in Hasa to attack Bahrain. The *Sphinx*, together with another ship, therefore crippled the Al-bin-Ali by destroying all their ships (44) in the harbour. Shortly after, the Turkish officials left, and Qasim had no option but to surrender. As a result of mediation, the entire Al-bin-Ali tribe, with the exception of its shaykh, agreed to return to Bahrain. Qasim was clearly defeated. To make matters worse, the British authorities threatened to destroy his fleet unless he paid a fine of 30,000 rupees; Qasim refused, and his dhows were destroyed.

But the defeat held unexpected gains. The British Government realised how close they had come to an armed conflict with the Ottomans, and wanted to make sure there would be no repetition of events. The Resident was consequently instructed to warn the ruler of Bahrain against interfering in the affairs of Qatar. This was, of course, an implicit recognition of the rights of the Al-Thani in Zubarah. At almost the same time, but without the knowledge of the warning to

Bahrain, Qasim sought to strengthen his hold on the town. He was successful in influencing those members of the Naim tribe who still lived in Zubarah to transfer their allegiance from the Al-Khalifah to the Al-Thani. From that date until 1937, no one officially questioned the ownership of Zubarah.

2. Qasim's Relations with the Ottomans: 1893

Although the crises over Zubarah went a long way to extending Qasim's rule over Qatar, his relationship with the Ottomans was, by and large, very strained. After they made him governor of Doha in 1879, he faced a period of internal lawlessness and resistance to his authority that he was at first powerless to counteract. The Bani Hajir tribe, for example, committed a number of piracies between 1874 and 1876, but the Ottoman presence in Doha prevented the British authorities from pressing for damages, and the illegalities went unpunished. Furthermore, the Al-bu-Kawarah tribe, annoyed at Qasim's alliance with the Turks, left Doha in 1879 and settled in Fuwayrat. There they were joined by members of the Naim tribe, the two elements combining to make the town defiant of Qasim's authority. Doha was also attacked several times by members of the Manasir and Awamir tribes, and in 1884 the imminence of an attack by the Ajman tribe was so great that no one dared to go to the pearl fisheries that season. But maybe the greatest threat to Qasim's internal authority occurred in 1885 when around 100 people from Wakrah left the town in order to escape Qasim's influence, settling in Ghariyah, on the north-eastern coast of Qatar. Although Qasim immediately attacked the town in an effort to reduce its power, its prestige grew when the son of the *wazir* of Bahrain, Muhammad bin Abdel Wahhab, whose sister was married to Muhammad bin Thani, became the shaykh of the town. His aim was to make Ghariyah independent of Qasim, and to do this he needed to win the favour of the Ottomans. This he accomplished by formally asking for the establishment of a Turkish customs post at Doha. The possibility of such an establishment at once angered and frightened Qasim, for not only would it have undermined his prestige, it would also have greatly reduced his personal income, much of which depended on customs dues. He reacted vigorously and managed to evict Muhammad and the inhabitants of Ghariyah from Qatar; but the damage was already done, for the possibility of a Turkish customs house in Doha still existed. Qasim therefore decided to leave Doha and renounce his authority over Qatar; he then systematically sought to create chaos in the town that would at one stroke cause the Ottomans to abandon their plans for a customs house and ask him to restore order. His plans did not succeed entirely. Although the Ottomans continued to recognise Qasim's position in Qatar, they landed a battalion of 250 Ottomans in Doha as a show of strength. They tried other means to obtain more direct control of Qatar, but these finally came to nothing; furthermore, despite Qasim's public announcement of having resigned his position as *Qaim Maqam*, the Ottomans refused to accept the resignation.

Another major problem that Qasim faced during this period was the bitter enmity of Zayid bin Khalifah of Abu Dhabi over al-Udayd. We have already noted the first secession of the Qubaysat section of the Bani Yas to al-Udayd from Abu Dhabi in 1835; the second, also short-lived, occurred in 1849 when the Qubaysat had hoped for a Wahhabi alliance. The third was in 1869, but after 1871, because of the Ottoman presence in Qatar, the situation became fraught with dangers of a wider nature. Although the Qubaysat refused to fly the Ottoman flag, they did pay tribute to the Turks, and in 1878 the Ottoman Foreign Minister claimed al-Udayd as part of Qatar. The British Government had earlier decided that it belonged to Abu Dhabi, but remained tacit on the question of sovereignty. To further complicate matters, both Qasim and Zayid laid claim to that place. Although the Qubaysat finally returned to Abu Dhabi in 1880, the resulting enmity between Qasim and Zayid grew in intensity with fierce raid and counter-raid between Qatar and Abu Dhabi becoming almost a regular habit. These reached a climax in 1888 when Qasim's son Ali was killed in battle outside Doha during an Abu Dhabi attack. Qasim's reaction both as a father and a ruler was to avenge the death of his son; he appealed to the Turks, to the other Trucial rulers and even to Ibn Rashid of Jabal Shammar. But the dangers of involvement with British ships of war prevented anyone coming to his aid, and Qasim was left to fight alone with a fortified Turkish garrison committed to protect Doha from further raids as his only support. With time, however, the tension abated, and Qasim was forced to focus his attention on more serious matters.

But he could not forget his resentment of the Ottomans for not having given him any material or moral assistance during his long conflict with Abu Dhabi, especially as they had also entered into an alliance, albeit short, with Muhammad bin Abdel Wahhab. He chafed at Ottoman domination, and grew increasingly reluctant to acknowledge it. His deliberate instigation of unrest in Doha acted in his favour, however, for it obstructed Ottoman plans to establish a customs house there, besides having put an end to the payments of tribute. The Ottomans, for their part, were angry at Qasim's treatment of their authority, and relations between the two began to deteriorate rapidly. Matters reached a head in February 1893, when the *vali* of Basra visited Doha to settle outstanding differences.

The visit was obviously important, for the *vali* was accompanied by a strong force made up of a regiment of infantry and over 300 cavalry. As soon as the Ottomans arrived in Doha, Qasim abruptly left the town and retired to Wajbah, 15 kilometres away. He had received information from Basra that part of the *vali's* mission was to take him prisoner, and he had also learned that the Ottoman troops were to be reinforced by a Kuwaiti force that had not yet arrived. Thus, when the *vali* sent for Qasim, the latter delegated his brother Ahmad as his emissary, claiming that he was too ill to make the journey. Letters between the *vali* and Qasim went back and forth for a month, with Ahmad serving as intermediary, but still Qasim refused to appear before the Ottoman official

The *vali* finally lost patience and decided to punish Qasim once and for all. Without any warning, he imprisoned Ahmad and sixteen of the leading men of Doha, and then proceeded to set up a blockade of the town both by sea and by land. He then made for Wajbah with his troops. Qasim by now feared that all was lost, but when the people of Wajbah, whom he had warned to leave the town before trouble befell them, resisted the entry of the Ottoman troops, he took heart. Despite his old age (he was probably close to eighty) he was still vigorous, and his fighting forces were well prepared, determined to stand up to the Ottomans. This they did, and fierce fighting ensued. The Qataris proved to be courageous and determined, undaunted by the obvious military superiority of their adversaries. Their determination was well rewarded and after one day it was clear that their forces had emerged victorious.[6] The Ottomans scurried back to Doha and, protected by a gunboat, shut themselves up in the fort there. The ship then fired its guns on the people of the town, but Qasim was not going to give up his victory now. He forced the *vali* to come to him for the safe return of the Ottoman cavalry to Hasa, in return for which he insisted on the liberation of Ahmad and the other incarcerated men of Doha. All of this Qasim achieved by controlling the water supply of the town, for the

Ottomans could not do without water. It goes without saying that the Kuwaiti force never entered Qatar.

The Ottoman defeat is a landmark in the modern history of Qatar, most of all because of the courage with which Qasim and his men faced up to the *vali*. Qasim's popularity and reputation in Qatar as a man of valour and strength grew further when the Ottomans had no choice but to grant him a full pardon. His authority was completely established, and although he chose to live in semi-retirement for the rest of his life, no one ever questioned his position as ruler. His brother, and later his sons, deputised for him in all matters that concerned relations with the Turks, but his decisions remained the most important. He had obviously done much for Qatar besides giving it a more independent status; he had also contributed to the beginning of its development as a state, instituting several social and economic measures to unify Qatar. Once his position was more secure throughout the peninsula, for example, he constructed roads to connect the main towns of Qatar. Furthermore, by the late nineteenth century, Qatar had ten *madrasahs* (religious schools) and one regular school that offered instruction up to the intermediary level.[7] Qasim moved to the oasis of Bu Hasa (Abu Hasiyyah), 20 kilometres inland from Lusail, after resigning from the Ottoman position of *Qaim Maqam*, and his brother Ahmad performed most of his duties for him in Doha,[8] his third son Abdel Rahman governing Wakrah after 1898. When, in 1905, Ahmad was murdered by his servant, Doha was governed by Abdallah, Qasim's fourth son.

The Ottomans continued to treat Qasim as *Qaim Maqam*, but their relationship with Qasim and Qatar was clearly at an end. The old man must have sensed the impending doom of the Ottoman Empire and directed his attention instead to the future. When, in 1902, Abdel Aziz bin Abdel Rahman Al-Saud (Ibn Saud), the grandson of Faysal bin Turki, took back Riyadh for the Wahhabis with a tiny group of followers, Qasim turned to him with pleasure. He became a Wahhabi by conviction,[9] and began an active relationship with Ibn Saud, sending him tribute and friendly assurances. He was fully aware of the effect his actions would have on the Ottomans, but did not concern himself with such problems. He rather saw the favourable impact that this new alliance would have on his strongly anti-Wahhabi enemy, the ruler of Abu Dhabi. Although Qasim was old by now and had badly impaired vision, he never lost his vigour.

In late 1905, the Political Agent in Bahrain went on his first visit to Qasim. On arriving at Bu Hasa, he noted with interest the well-laid-out garden; lined with tamarisk trees, it had large plots of lucerne grass,

pomegranate trees and at least 300 date trees. Qasim, he found to be
'a patriarch of the ancient type' with a long grey beard who looked
much younger than his age. The octogenarian was clearly an overpower-
ing figure, proudly displaying a six-year-old son and, when amused,
breaking into 'infectious roars of laughter'. He was very friendly and
hospitable to the Englishman, and showed much interest in politics
although he professed to have been retired.[10]

3. The Turning Point: 1913

Twenty years after the Ottoman defeat in Qatar, three events occurred
that were to be significant to the modern development of the state,
marking the end of an era and ushering in a new and totally different
situation. The first of these was in May 1913 when the resurgent
Wahhabis, under the leadership of Ibn Saud, reconquered the Hasa
province of eastern Arabia from the Ottomans. This at one stroke
brought the Wahhabis into the forefront of Gulf politics, a position
they retain today, and ended the domination of the peninsula by
the Ottoman Turks. Two months later, in July 1913, the old Qasim
died, and his son Abdullah, who had governed Doha since 1905, became
the next ruler of Qatar. The third event was the unratified (because of
the outbreak of World War I) Anglo-Turkish Convention of 19 July
1913 whereby the Ottoman Empire renounced all rights to Qatar,
thus formally ending their occupation of the peninsula. Two days after
the conclusion of the Anglo-Turkish Convention, the Shaykh of Bahrain
tried to revive his right to levy tribute from Qatar according to the
terms of the 1868 treaty. But Article 10 of the Convention protected
Qatar from having to pay the money: 'Le Governement de sa Majesté
Britannique déclare qu'il ne permettra pas au cheikh de Bahreine de
s'immiser dans les affaires intérieures d'El Katr.' And so the ruler of
Bahrain was duly informed.[11]

Qatar was now well on the way to forming two new relationships
that cancelled and replaced its ties of the nineteenth century with
Bahrain and the Ottoman Empire; the first was with the Wahhabis,
the second with the British Government. Both were important, each
one having had a precedent in the nineteenth century. The Wahhabi
link with Qatar was based on geographical reasons, the undefined
desert boundaries between Hasa and Qatar often coming to nothing in
the face of a strong force in the former place. The British ties, like
those with the Wahhabis, had existed informally in the nineteenth
century. During the first half of the twentieth century, however, the
British presence in the Gulf, and consequently in Qatar, far outweighed

that of the Wahhabis in importance, power and prestige.

Qasim's relationship with the British authorities had always been strained. One of the most important sources for the trouble was Qasim's treatment of Indian residents in Qatar. All Indians living in the Gulf enjoyed special privileges as British subjects. They were wont to abuse these privileges, and were consequently resented by the local inhabitants. They had settled in the region primarily to take part in the pearl trade, and many of them were much wealthier than the local people, thus enjoying the upper hand in the complicated system of debts around which the trade revolved. Since Qasim was not bound by formal treaty relations to Britain and since the latter could not impose its authority on him during the period of Ottoman occupation, it was precisely during this period that his mistreatment of the Indians reached its height. Qasim himself was a pearl trader of major importance, the Indians thus regarding him as a business competitor, and he seized the opportunity to impose his own regulations on them almost immediately after he was named *Qaim Maqam*. In 1883, he expelled them and closed their shops in Doha. But the British Government could not allow these events to go unpunished. Despite Ottoman remonstrances which finally came to nothing, the Political Resident went to Doha and threatened Qasim with British guns if the ruler refused to formally apologise to the British Government for the insult to British subjects and pay compensation to the traders; he also had to allow them to return. Realising he had no other choice, Qasim complied; this made him even more bitter with the Indians. When, during the period referred to above, Qasim left Doha to escape the possibility of a Turkish customs house, the ensuing lawlessness damaged much of the trade of the resident Indians, to say nothing of their personal safety. Once again, Qasim was forced to pay compensation, and because a number of Bahrainis in Doha had also suffered considerable losses, causing the ruler of Bahrain to complain to the Political Resident, the latter ordered that goods worth 10,000 rupees belonging to Qasim in Bahrain be impounded as partial compensation. Once again, there were strong Ottoman protests to the British Government that came to nothing, and Qasim found himself with no choice but to pay even more compensation yet again. During the disturbances, an emissary sent by the Resident to Doha arranged for the evacuation of the Indians from that place; they were not to return, and Qatar consequently became the only Gulf shaykhdom until the recent past without an Indian community.

Despite Qatar's stormy relations with the British Government, the Al-Thani were well aware of the advantages of a British alliance if for nothing else but as a useful means to shed the Ottoman yoke, particularly after the latter had obviously been unwilling to defend Qasim. In 1902, for example, Qasim's brother approached the Assistant Political Agent in Bahrain.[12] He referred to the fact that he held the water and supplies of Doha at his mercy and could turn the Ottomans out if the British government so wished. He was clearly anxious to obtain the protection of the British government, and the Political Resident in Bushire recommended acceptance of Ahmad's proposal to the Government of India.[13] But the British Ambassador in Constantinople, who saw the maintenance of Anglo-Turkish relations as far more important, vehemently opposed the suggestion.

In 1905, the Political Agent in Bahrain, after a visit to Qatar, reported that Ahmad had not requested a British treaty; he discovered, to his surprise, that the 1902 meeting with Ahmad had been misunderstood, and that Ahmad had in reality only wanted British permission to settle in Zubarah. Whether the Assistant Political Agent in 1902 had misunderstood Ahmad's message or whether Ahmad had in fact changed his mind three years later, the Al-Thani had definitely altered their attitude towards the British after 1893. And although the Government of India was anxious to formalise its relationship with Qatar, it had to accept the Foreign Office's objections regarding Anglo-Ottoman relations. It was not until 1913 that all the previous constraints were removed; three years later, the Anglo-Qatari agreement was signed.

Notes

1. The Ottoman administrative districts were a *vilayet* (province) governed by a *vali*; a *sanjak* (sub-province) governed by a *mutasarrif*; a *qada* (district) governed by a *qaim maqam*, and a *nahiye* governed by a *mudir*.

2. J. G. Lorimer *Gazeteer of the Persian Gulf, 'Oman and Central Arabia,* 5 vols. (Calcutta, 1908-15, republished by Gregg International, Westmead, UK, 1970), vol. I, p. 809.

3. For an account of Anglo-Ottoman rivalry in the Gulf during this period, see Briton C. Busch, *Britain and the Persian Gulf, 1894-1914* (Berkeley, California, 1967).

4. Ali had been killed by Muhammad bin Khalifah, and it was through British intervention that Isa became ruler.

5. R/15/1/314: Pol. Res. to Govt of India, 11 July 1895 (tele.). The entire incident is described in this volume.

6. Much of the details of the account of the battle have been drawn from Mahmud Bahjat Sinan, *Tarikh Qatar al-Am* (Baghdad, 1966), pp. 93-5.

7. Ibid., p. 91.

8. Qasim had apparently wanted his son Muhammad to perform these duties, but the elders of Qatar preferred Ahmad. He told the Assistant Political Agent in Bahrain in 1903 that the Turks had accepted his 'abdication' since 1898. R/15/2/27: Asst Pol. Agent Bahrain to Asst Pol. Res., 20 September 1903.

9. Qasim was a Maliki Sunni by birth. Sometime during the late nineteenth century he had changed to the Hanbali sect, bringing his tribe into spiritual proximity with the Wahhabis.

10. R/15/2/26: Pol. Agent Bahrain to Pol. Res., 23 December 1905.

11. R/15/2/30: No. 1704 EA Confidential, 31 July 1913.

12. R/15/2/26: Gaskin, Asst Pol. Agent, Bahrain to C. A. Kemball, Pol. Res., 22 March 1902.

13. Ibid., Pol. Res. to Govt of India, 16 April 1902.

5 THE TREATY OF 1916 AND ITS AFTERMATH

1. The Treaty of 1916

The renaissance of the Wahhabi movement that had lain dormant since 1871 began after Ibn Saud captured Riyadh. As he started the establishment of the *Ikhwan* as the backbone of his forces, the British Government was more concerned with other events in the peninsula, namely the Arab Revolt under the leadership of the Sharifian dynasty of the Hijaz. It was not until May 1913 when the Saudi forces captured Hasa and Ibn Saud's cousin, Abdallah bin Jaluwi, was named governor of the province that the Wahhabi movement was brought into direct contact with the Gulf and its British representatives there for the first time in the twentieth century. Almost immediately afterwards, in December 1913, the Political Resident warned Ibn Saud not to interfere with the shaykhdoms in treaty relations with Britain. The British authorities were well aware of the significance of the nearby Wahhabi presence on places like Qatar and the Trucial Coast. The Political Resident had voiced his fears of the effects of this specifically on Qatar: 'I have not a doubt that Bin Saud could eat up Qatar in a week and I am rather afraid that he may do so.'[1] Qasim had also realised this, and had started to fear the Wahhabi leader the year before his death. In 1915, Ibn Saud officially committed himself in a treaty with Britain to abstain from interfering in the affairs of the states on the Arab side of the Gulf:

> Bin Saud undertakes, as his father did before him, to refrain from all aggression on, or interference with the territories of Kuwait, Bahrain, and of the Shaikhs of Qatar and the Oman Coast, who are under the protection of the British Government, and who have treaty relations with the said Government; and the limits of their territories shall be hereafter determined.[2]

The next year the guns of World War I began to fire, with Britain and the Ottoman Empire on opposite sides. Abdallah bin Qasim cast his lot with the British and sent the Political Resident his wishes for success and victory. He had obviously backed the right horse, for in 1915 the Ottomans abandoned Doha, leaving behind three guns, 500 shells and 105,000 rounds of ammunition.

The field was now open for Britain. It could, without the old pre-war worries of endangering its relations with the Porte, conclude an agreement with the clearly independent Qatar. But Abdallah's position was a weak one, and he was very hesitant about the outcome of such a treaty. Here it must be mentioned that, in 1905, Abdallah had been very reluctant to become governor of Doha following Ahmad's death; he had at first refused the position, saying he was much more interested in continuing his work as a pearl merchant, but at his father's insistence he finally assumed the governorship. Even then he encountered a fair amount of opposition from his immediate family. He had no less than twelve brothers, the eldest of whom, Khalifah, was probably the most difficult to deal with. Qasim had been able to keep his sons under control, but after his death Abdallah was often at a loss to cope with his dissident brothers, to say nothing of his cousins, the sons of Ahmad.[3]

Consequently the negotiations for the conclusions of the treaty lasted for one year. Abdallah's brothers regarded it as a replacement of the hated Turkish relationship, so the ruler was very worried about the local impact of certain clauses. He particularly feared the reaction to one of the clauses that admitted British subjects into Qatar, since the memory of the Indian traders was still strong in Qatari minds. The Political Resident gradually gave in to many of Abdallah's requests and the agreement was finally signed on 3 November 1916 between Abdallah and Percy Cox, the Political Resident.

It placed Qatar on much the same footing as the Trucial shaykhdoms who had signed the same agreement in 1892, for in it, the ruler undertook not to cede, sell, lease or mortgage any of his territory without British consent; not to have relations with any foreign power without British consent; to accept the establishment of post and telegraph offices; to admit British subjects to Qatar and to protect them; to accept the stationing at Doha of a British agent if Britain desired it; and to desist from piracy, the slave trade and arms traffic.[4] The treaty 'was, in fact, a combination of every sort of restrictive treaty concluded by Britain in the Gulf over the previous century and placed Qatar firmly within the British orbit'.[5] The concessions made to ensure Abdallah's signature were as follows: the articles concerning a British agent (Article VIII), British postal and telegraphic offices (Article IX), and the protection of British residents (Article VII) were to remain inoperative for the time being, since Abdallah did not feel sufficiently strong internally to impose them on his people.[6] Also, the ruler and his family were allowed to retain the slaves in their possession provided they were treated with justice. But one major exception to the treaties that had bound Kuwait, Bahrain, Abu Dhabi, Dubai, Sharjah, Ajman, and

Umm al-Qaiwain to Britain during the nineteenth century was included, for Abdallah was clearly unwilling to commit himself to the British Government without receiving assurances of extra protection. Hitherto, the only form of defence granted the other shaykhdoms in the various treaties by Britain was the undertaking to foil any attack by sea. Abdallah insisted on the inclusion of an extra clause in the agreement, one that would assure him of protection from land attacks. This was Article XI, which stated as follows: 'They [the British Government] also undertake to grant me good offices, should I or my subjects be assailed by land within the territories of Qatar.'[7] Although Abdallah obviously relied on Article XI, he would have been startled to know that, in the words of an India Office Memorandum, it 'did not . . . in practice impose any very serious liability on His Majesty's Government.'[8]

Abdallah bin Qasim was recognised as the independent ruler of Qatar, and was accordingly granted the title of CIE (Companion of the Most Eminent Order of the Indian Empire) and a seven-gun salute in 1919. Yet his treaty relations did little to secure a stable position for him. Until his usefulness was recognised when the scramble for oil concessions first began seriously in the 1930s, he was subjected to a most unusual series of chilling rebuffs by British authorities. Many of them are difficult to fathom. The British authorities in Bushire, Delhi and London were loathe to become involved in Qatar or its affairs, at the same time wishing to obtain and remain in control of the shaykhdom. The cost of fending off involvement sometimes became an exercise in polemics. British officials in India and at home subjected the articles of the 1916 treaty to tortuous interpretations and re-interpretations, each argument depending on the specific issue at stake.

2. Interpretations of the Treaty

A significant feature of British policy in the Gulf, one that Abdallah was soon to learn from experience as had his fellow rulers, was the consistent inconsistency with which treaty regulations were interpreted. Despite the existence of mutual agreements whereby Britain was also bound to offer protection in the case of an attack by sea, these binding clauses could often, if necessary, be argued away. In 1928, for example, a Dubai ship was subjected to severe mishandling by the Iranian navy with the result that the people of Dubai and other Trucial shaykhdoms were prepared to launch an expedition to avenge their relatives and friends, particularly when no tangible help seemed to be forthcoming from the British authorities. The latter, in the person of the Political

Resident, reacted with great firmness: he reminded the people of their treaty obligations to desist from maritime warfare, knowing at the same time that the only counter-measures being taken were diplomatic protests to Tehran. In the words of a Treasury official in London, the British Government, 'by saving them from such a rash act [as allowing the expedition against Iran to take place] we have done them [the Arabs of the Trucial Coast] another good service.'[9] When the possibility of providing compensation for the losses incurred by the victims of the vessel was discarded by the British Government in London, a Foreign Office official explained: 'We have reluctantly come to the conclusion that the relationship of these Arabs towards us is not such as to justify them in expecting compensation from us.'[10]

Abdallah was not spared this kind of problem. In 1921, he confidentially asked A. P. Trevor, the Political Resident, to visit him in Doha. When Trevor arrived, Abdallah pressed him for specifications about the various forms of security he could expect from Britain. Would he receive help if he were to be attacked from the interior of Qatar; if any portion of the shaykhdom were to rise against him; or if one of his brothers (namely Khalifah, his older brother) were to threaten his authority by attempting to overthrow him?[11] The first of the three contingencies was an oblique reference to the possible extension of Wahhabi interests in Qatar, for Abdallah was not willing to acknowledge any hostility between himself and Ibn Saud. He was quick to assure Trevor that he was on the very best terms with the King, 'but that times were uncertain, Bin Saud might be killed or die, or his followers get out of hand etc.'[12] But Trevor could not even reassure Abdallah. He told him that, in the event of a Wahhabi attack, the most he could expect from Britain would be diplomatic help. That, he explained to the startled Abdallah, was the true meaning of Article XI that had promised the ruler the 'good offices' of Britain in case of attack by land. It must be noted here that more than one contemporary interpretation of Article XI, made without having had recourse to British records such as the Trevor despatch quoted here, also assumed that the 1916 treaty gave the ruler of Qatar protection in the case of attack by land.[13] It would not be unrealistic to assume, therefore, that Abdallah thought so as well, or that Cox might have tacitly encouraged him to believe it in order to obtain his signature.

Regarding the possibility of an attack from within Qatar, and the threat from Abdallah's brothers, Trevor's view was 'that Government would not be able to see their way to assisting since, as he [Abdallah] knew, their policy is to interfere as little as possible in internal affairs.'[14]

So on all fronts, Trevor could offer little to strengthen Abdallah's position as ruler. Abdallah had also asked Trevor for two other items: first, he needed to borrow money, and second, he wanted a couple of small guns. When the Resident questioned him closely about the loan, he discovered that Abdallah was truly impecunious. This was largely due to his inability to collect customs dues — at that time one of the few means a ruler had to maintain a Treasury — because of the great prevailing insecurity of the Doha customs, another result of the misbehaviour of the Al-Thani brothers. When Abdallah admitted there was little likelihood that he could repay a loan, he dropped the matter, and took up the question of the guns instead. Although Trevor assured him that the British Government did not usually supply guns, the Resident obviously felt the time had come to make concessions. He privately told the Government of India that if they could find some obsolete guns, their presence in Qatar would go a long way to ensuring some form of internal peace for Abdallah. The answer to Trevor from India is interesting. No precedent could be found for giving guns to any ruler of the Gulf littoral, but if Abdallah were to stop all traces of gun-running, which apparently prevailed in Qatar, 'the gift of two unserviceable guns with a supply of blank ammunition might be considered if artillery limited to ceremonial use seemed . . . to meet the case.'[15] That, in the final analysis, was all the help given to Abdallah for the time being.

But the ruler was persistent and would not leave the matter there. He was very disturbed about his own insecurity, and tried again to obtain British help a few months later. This time he went to Bahrain, ostensibly to sell pearls, but in reality to consult with the Political Agent there on his problems. During the conversation, Abdallah reminded the Agent that the object of Ibn Saud's attempt to undermine his influence at home was to place Qatar under his protection. Ibn Saud was now deliberately courting all the disaffected members of the ruling family who openly defied Abdallah's authority. The ruler of Qatar warned the Agent that he would soon be unable to retain his position, and rather than submit to Saudi suzerainty, he and his son would leave Qatar.

Abdallah, however, had plans of his own. He wanted to reassert his authority and needed to know from the Political Agent to what extent he could rely on British support. A few coastal villages, for example, were actively resisting his authority by refusing to pay tribute and by fighting amongst themselves. He wanted to subdue them by attacking them with a naval force, and wished to know if the British Government would waive the regulations about maritime hostilities for that express purpose. Abdallah also wanted to ascertain if, in case he did attack these villages and in case Wahhabi forces would rally to their support, the British Government would protect him from attack by sea according to treaty obligations. Finally, he asked that the British Government formally recognise his son Hamad as his heir, for he needed a powerful tool with which to fight his enemies.[16]

But Abdallah was to be disappointed again. The Agent in Bahrain was requested to tell the ruler that 'the Government of India do not desire to get mixed up in the internal affairs of Qatar, and will only assist the Shaikh against Bin Saud by diplomatic means.'[17] All naval attacks constituted a breach of the maritime peace to which Abdallah had pledged himself in the 1916 treaty, but no notice would be taken if the ruler were to use boats in order to preserve order; in case of a spread in fighting, however, Abdallah could not rely on British help because it would not be a case of aggression by outsiders, but rather opposition by recalcitrant subjects.

The Political Resident realised the gravity of Abdallah's position and remarked with sympathy 'I think it would be a pity if Qatar disappeared as a separate entity.'[18] But he was clearly convinced that no direct action was called for. All he could suggest was that the British Government write to Ibn Saud and ask him to restrain his people from all forms of aggression in Qatar which was in treaty relations with Britain. This was done, and the Resident did not concern himself with the problem for the rest of his term in office.

In 1932, Abdallah tried yet again to obtain protection, this time putting the request in the form of a bargain. The Royal Air Force, who were in the process of setting up an imperial air route from England to India, were at the time relying very heavily on the Arab coast of the Gulf for storage and landing facilities.[19] They were particularly interested in finding an emergency landing ground in Doha, so the Political Agent went to Qatar first to see if a suitable place could be found and then to sound out the ruler for permission. The Agent arrived in April and found that Abdallah would only discuss a landing site in exchange for further support from the British Government, particularly if his borders needed protection.[20] The ruler put forward his case simply: he could never guarantee the safety of the landing ground with the continuing state of lawlessness in Qatar. After some thought, the Political Resident, who obviously concurred, came up with a solution: he decided to send two letters to the Political Agent to take to Abdallah, the first granting the ruler protection only in Doha, the second granting it to him in Doha and along the coast. The Agent was instructed to offer the ruler the first one in exchange for granting RAF facilities; if he refused it, then he could have the second one.[21]

The Agent went to Doha in August and found Abdallah in a difficult mood. He did not want to irritate the ruler unduly, so he offered him the second letter straight away. Abdallah surprised him by rejecting it because it was signed by the Political Resident and not by the Viceroy of India. Abdallah clearly wanted to avoid accepting what seemed to him a mere repetition of the 1916 promises that had been made by a Political Resident and that carried no weight. This rebuff infuriated the Political Resident. He wrote to the ruler telling him that after 1 October 1932, aeroplanes would begin to fly over Qatar; if they were forced to land there, Abdallah was expected to give them assistance and he would be rewarded; if Abdallah were to show hostility, he would be held personally responsible.[22] This answer cut short any further possibility of protection, but, three years later, Abdallah was to find another means to obtain what he desired.

3. The British Position

Abdallah's inability to extract any concessions from the Political Resident was a strong indication of the new situation arising from the 1916 treaty. Although, for example, his grandfather had once welcomed the advent of Faysal bin Turki in order to weaken the hold of Bahrain over Qatar, Abdallah now feared the threat of Wahhabi domination over Qatar. Bahrain no longer held any but minimal claims to the Qatar peninsula, and Britain, with whom Abdallah had entered into treaty relations, was obviously unwilling to become in any way involved in his internal affairs.

The British position had changed as well. Once the Turkish presence on the eastern coast of Arabia had been removed by the disintegration of the Ottoman Empire, Britain could pursue a more forceful policy in Qatar. The 1916 treaty had placed the shaykhdom firmly within the British orbit and had neutralised the manoeuvring ability of its ruler. But Qatar was not alone in being constrained by British ties; all the other states on the Arab shores of the Gulf had attained a similar status after World War I.

During the latter part of the nineteenth century, British policy in the Gulf had had to contend with the growing rivalry of other powers. The French government had competed for control of the Sultanate of Muscat and Oman, virtually ended by the Anglo-French Entente of 1904; and the Russians had opposed the British presence in the Gulf, once again removed by the Anglo-Russian Convention of 1907. But the German policy of *Drang nach Osten*, which culminated in the project of the Berlin-Baghdad railway with a terminus in Kuwait, and the Ottoman presence in Qatar had presented the greatest threats to British supremacy. With the defeat of Germany and the collapse of the Ottoman Empire after World War I, the Gulf emerged in 1919 as an uncontested British lake. But there were additional responsibilities and involvements. Britain had occuped Iraq during the war and, soon after, secured a mandate there. After 1913, Ibn Saud's territory extended to the Gulf, thus bringing him into a new relationship with the British Government. British interests had also increased with official British control of the Anglo-Persian Oil Company in 1914 after the discovery of oil in commercial quantities in southern Persia. They had also grown with the strategic plans to develop an air route from England to India that would pass through the Gulf. Thus the Gulf region could no longer remain the primary concern of India alone; its importance was recognised by Britain and its empire as a whole. With time, two new countries gained importance in Gulf politics, the newly formed Saudi Arabia and the Iran of Riza Shah. Both states were gradually to disturb the *status quo* of the British position, the former by its spectacular growth that finally encompassed most of the Arabian peninsula and the latter by its militant nationalism against British domination; this was reflected in the many attempts to assert Persian sovereignty over various islands in the Gulf, including Bahrain. Last, but by no means least, the possibility of the existence of petroleum resources gave rise to the British policy to channel these resources into British-owned companies.

The situation in the Gulf thus brought about certain changes in the exercise of British power. The Residency at Bushire had been established in 1763. Until 1873, responsibility had been first with the East India Company and then the Government of Bombay. After that date, the political control of the Gulf had been exercised primarily by the Government of India. In 1878, the Political Resident also became Consul-General for Fars, Khuzistan, Luristan and Persian islands in the Gulf. Thus the position had dual responsibilities: to the Government of India for the Political Residency and to the Foreign Office in London for the Consulate-General. The cost of the Residency was also shared by the two bodies. Officers of the Indian Political Service, known as Political Agents, stationed in Muscat (from 1800), Bahrain (from 1900 as Assistant and from 1904 as Political Agent), and Kuwait (from 1904) were subordinate to the Political Resident.

The headquarters at Bushire in southern Persia of the British command in the Gulf also underwent change. After the rise to power of Riza Khan (later, Shah) in Persia in 1921, British privileges in the country began to recede. One of the first acts of Riza Khan's government had been to denounce the Anglo-Persian Agreement of 1919 that had placed Britain in control of Persian finances and its army. As the Persian Government made it increasingly clear that it would not be willing to accept foreign, to say nothing of British, domination, the prestige and control of Britain there began to wane. The Arab side of the Gulf thus started to assume greater importance *vis-à-vis* British interests, and in 1936 it was decided to move the Political Residency away from Bushire and to Bahrain,[23] a strong indication of the new centre of gravity for British control of the Gulf.

Until 1921, the Resident, as such, was responsible to the Government of India. After that date, as a result of the British mandates in Iraq and Palestine and increased British involvement with the Sharifian dynasty in the Hijaz and with Ibn Saud, the control of policy in the Gulf was transferred from India to London. This was first exercised by the newly established Middle East Department in the Colonial Office and after 1929 decisions were made by an Inter-Departmental Committee (which included members of the Foreign Office, Colonial Office, the India Office, the War Office, the Air Ministry and the Admiralty), a recognition of the wider range that Gulf affairs had assumed within the Near Eastern political framework. In 1933, the India Office assumed the functions previously performed by the Colonial Office with reference to the Gulf. The role of the Government of India became confined to administrative and local matters, all the officers in the Gulf continuing to be recruited from its service.

These officers wielded great power locally. Most important, of course, was the Political Resident who was once referred to as the uncrowned king of the Gulf. By 1900, the position had become one of paramount influence and authority, strengthened in 1904 by the presence of Sir Percy Cox, who remained in office for over a decade. It was Cox who negotiated the treaty with Abdallah. Despite the fact that he had by then also become Chief Political Officer of the Indian Expeditionary Force in Mesopotamia, it was clear that the unique relationship he had established with the rulers in the Gulf made it essential that Cox alone could be entrusted with business of this sort. He therefore left Baghdad for Doha in order to ensure the completion of the treaty. The next Resident to attain a position similar to that of Cox was Lt Col. T. C. W. Fowle who remained in office from 1932 to 1939. He came to the position with a lifetime of experience behind him, and within a short time became a well known and respected figure in Gulf politics.[24]

Of the three Political Agents – in Kuwait, Muscat and Bahrain – it was the latter who had the largest responsibility. He was not only in charge of Bahrain affairs; he also oversaw events in Abu Dhabi, Dubai, Sharjah, Umm al-Qaiwain, Ras al-Khaimah, Ajman and Kalba. After 1928, Qatar was included in his area of responsibility. In the case of the Trucial States, the Political Agent could rely on the work of a Residency Agent, a local Arab stationed in Sharjah; the Residency Agent deputised for the Political Agent who thus only needed to visit the Trucial States on matters of outstanding importance. But Qatar had no similar agent, and the Bahrain Agency Files have very scanty information on Qatar. Once the oil concession was about to be signed in Qatar, however, both the Resident and the Agent began to pay frequent visits to the peninsula.

Over and above these officers, the Senior Naval Officer of the Persian Gulf Division played a very important role. He often performed the practical duties of a Political Agent, thus becoming well acquainted with the rulers and their problems. Above all, however, he represented the instrument of power by which Britain controlled the Gulf. He was well informed on local affairs, for it was through him that the constant interchange of intelligence was channelled. He co-ordinated policy with the Admiralty, the India Office and the Government of India; his ships, of course, policed the waters of the Gulf.

Thus, for all the Arab coast there were only three Agents and a Resident living there permanently, with the six sloops that made up the Persian Gulf Division cruising nearby. Yet the control was absolute and the strategical, political and commercial interests for Britain enormous. British achievements were many, to quote the words of the Political Resident in 1938:

> we pay no subsidies to any Shaikhs . . . We raise no tribal levies . . . We do not maintain a single soldier or policeman on the whole of the Arab side . . . Our expenses and commitments are in fact limited to one Resident, three Political Agents and their office staffs![25]

Notes

1. R/15/2/30: Knox to Keyes (Pol. Agent, Bahrain), 15 September 1913.
2. C. U. Aitchison, *A Collection of Treaties, Engagements and Sanads Relating to India and Neighbouring Countries* (Delhi, 1933), vol. XI, p. 208.
3. R/15/2/30: See extracts from Yusuf bin Ahmad Kanoo's news reports on the Al-Thani, 1912-1914, July/August 1914. Kanoo supplied the Political Agent

in Bahrain with most of the information about Qatar.

4. R/15/2/30: Sir P. Z. Cox to Govt of India, 4 November 1916. The treaty is in Aitchison, *Collection of Treaties*, pp. 258-61. See Appendix III.

5. Briton C. Busch, *Britain and the Persian Gulf, 1894-1914* (California, 1967), p. 347.

6. This was included in a subsidiary letter from Cox to Abdallah. R/15/2/30, Cox to Govt of India, 4 November 1916 (translation enclosed).

7. Aitchison, *Collection of Treaties*, p. 260. See Appendix II.

8. L/P & S/18: B.402: 'El Ka?r, 1908-1916', 5 September 1928.

9. L/P & S/10: P. 4535/1928[2]: P. 3034/1929: A. P. Waterfield (Treasury) to Monteagle (Foreign Office), 3 April 1919 (copy). For an account of the entire incident, see Rosemarie J. Said, 'The role of Britain in the conflict over the Tunb Islands, 1928-1971' (in Arabic), *Journal of Gulf and Arabian Peninsula Studies*, vol. 2, no. 6 (April 1976).

10. L/P & S/10: P. 4535/1928[2]: P. 5769: Rendel (FO) to Walton (India Office), 2 September 1929.

11. L/P & S/11/222: P. 5027/22: Trevor to D. de S. Bray (Govt of India) 13 May 1921.

12. Ibid.

13. Husain M. Al-Baharna, *The Legal Status of the Arabian Gulf States* (Manchester, 1968), p. 39; Busch, *Britain and the Persian Gulf*, pp. 346-7.

14. L/P & S/11/222: P. 5027/22: Trevor (Pol. Res.) to D. de S. Bray (Govt of India), 13 May 1921.

15. Ibid., Govt of India to Pol. Res., 8 August 1921.

16. Ibid., P. 5027/22: Trevor to D. de S. Bray, 10 November 1922.

17. Ibid.

18. Ibid.

19. For an account of the setting up of the air route, see Rosemarie Said Zahlan, *The Origins of the United Arab Emirates* (London, 1978), Chapter 6.

20. R/15/2/141, Pol. Agent to Pol. Res., 30 May 1932.

21. Ibid. Pol. Res. to Pol. Agent., 12 August 1932. Two letters enclosed.

22. Ibid., Pol. Res. to Shaykh Abdallah, 22 September 1932 (translation).

23. This was finally accomplished in 1947.

24. For an account of the duties of the British officers in the Gulf, see Said Zahlan, *Origins of the United Arab Emirates*, Chapter 11.

25. L/P & S/12/3747: P. Z. 4113/38: Fowle (Pol. Res.) to Metcalfe (Govt of India), 23 May 1938.

6   THE PRELIMINARY OIL CONCESSION, 1935

1. The Procedures

It is difficult today to think of the Arab shaykhdoms of the Gulf without their large petroleum reserves; it is even more difficult perhaps to revive the mood of both parties, the company and the ruler, when the preliminary oil concessions were being signed in the 1930s. Maybe the most unusual feature is the fact that few if any of the British officials concerned at the time — in London, Delhi or the Gulf — really believed in the possibility of the existence of oil in commercial quantities in the Gulf shaykhdoms. Even when oil was struck in Bahrain in 1932, it seemed to have been regarded as an isolated fact, little thought having been given to the same event occurring in neighbouring places. British oil policy in the Gulf was slow in being formulated. Problems were dealt with as they arose, the discovery of oil having been one of the least important contingencies. In fact, had United States oil companies not evinced an interest in all of eastern Arabia, it is unlikely that preliminary concessions in Kuwait, Qatar, Abu Dhabi and the other Trucial States would have been signed during the 1930s.

The best illustration of this fact is the rather unusual story of Frank Holmes, the mining engineer from New Zealand, who, immediately after World War I, foresaw the great petroleum potential of Arabia with almost prophetic insight. In 1920, with little capital and few believers, he registered the Eastern and General Syndicate in London, a company that would buy oil concessions from Arabia and then sell them to the larger companies. In 1922, he attended the Conference of Uqayr (between the British government and Ibn Saud to delineate the borders of Iraq and Jordan with Nejd) and personally impressed Ibn Saud, who granted him a concession in 1923 despite British opposition. For four years Holmes tried unsuccessfully to interest oil companies to buy the Saudi concession; finally, his financial losses were so great that he was forced to discontinue the contract. In the meantime, he obtained for Eastern and General an option for Bahrain which he managed to sell to the California Standard Oil Company (Socal) after the Iraq Petroleum Company (IPC), who had priority to oil rights in Bahrain by the Red Line Agreement of 1928,[1] had turned down the offer. The Bahrain Petroleum Company (Bapco) was thus formed. When Bapco struck oil in May 1932, Socal acted quickly and, despite the competition of the British-controlled IPC, obtained a concession from Ibn Saud the next year.

The die was cast. The British Government was no longer content to sit by and watch American companies in Arabia. It wanted to ensure that only British companies entered the field. Qatar was no exception, particularly as Article V of the 1916 treaty specified that the ruler could not grant a concession without the approval of the British Government. The procedure for the preliminary concession was as follows: an exploratory option was generally granted to a company by a ruler for a specific amount of time; the object of the option was the right of that company to negotiate for an oil concession within the prescibed amount of time.

In 1922, Holmes had tried to obtain an exploratory option from Abdallah bin Qasim, convinced that Qatar held great possibilities in terms of petroleum resources. The Political Agent in Bahrain, however, persuaded Abdallah to turn away from Holmes, and in March 1926 he granted an option to the D'Arcy Exploration Company, a subsidiary of the Anglo-Persian Oil Company (APOC), instead. Under the terms of the Red Line Agreement, APOC could not operate concessions in Qatar except in conjunction with its other partners in IPC. So it was planned that when Abdallah granted a concession to APOC, the latter would transfer its rights in the options to a new subsidiary created for that purpose, Petroleum Concessions (Qatar) Ltd. Petroleum Concessions Ltd (PCL) was formed and registered in London in 1935. All its shares were held by the same interests and in the same proportion as the IPC except for the fact that there was to be no Iraqi representative on the Board. Affiliates of PCL such as Petroleum Concessions (Qatar) Ltd could then be created in different countries.

It is clear from all the evidence available that Abdallah was at first totally unaware of the undreamed-of prosperity that lay ahead for Qatar with respect to oil. He agreed to renew the D'Arcy option just before it expired on more than one occasion. At last, the final date of the option was set for August 1934, and still there were no signs of the possibility of a concession. It was during 1933 that the British authorities, not least Fowle, the Political Resident, began to be aware of the strong rivalry of Socal in the Gulf. The generous terms of the latter, in striking contrast with those offered by the IPC for the same agreement, had enabled it to win the concession from Ibn Saud. In the words of an official who negotiated with Ibn Saud on behalf of the IPC in 1933, the British company 'would speak only of rupees when gold was demanded'.[2] News of the gold that Socal was paying Ibn Saud soon reached the shaykhdoms of the Gulf. The rulers thus became more aware of the commercial possibilities of oil concessions and were clearly loath to sign away these chances to the APOC and its meagre offers. Abdallah was no exception. To make matters worse for Fowle, he began to hear that Socal, from its offices in Saudi Arabia and Bahrain, was quietly beginning to send out emissaries to the different rulers. Fowle was particularly suspicious about Holmes, the *eminence grise* of British officialdom in the Gulf, who was rumoured to be in contact with Abdallah bin Qasim and attempting to dissuade him from APOC.

There were other problems as well. The fear that Ibn Saud himself was behind Socal loomed large, and posed a constant threat to British interests. Furthermore, the question of how to manage the concession, if and when obtained, became a subject of much discussion in the various government departments in London. It was Fowle who was able to resolve all the outstanding conflicts and who was instrumental in formulating a Qatar oil policy; and it was largely due to his efforts that the APOC was to acquire the best commercial terms possible.

2. The Discussions

There were three concurrent sets of discussions taking place between 1933 and 1935 regarding the Qatar oil treaty. The first was between officials of the India Office and Foreign Office in London regarding policy in Qatar. The second was between Abdallah and Fowle. And the third, often interdependent on the outcome of the previous two, was between APOC and Abdallah. It is interesting to note that certain stringent forms of control over Abdallah were seriously contemplated in London when it seemed clear that APOC was at last about to secure its concession. When, however, the chances for APOC began to grow dimmer day by day, all earlier such thoughts were discarded, and Abdallah was at last able to secure what he had been pleading for since 1921.

The two most important points of policy that were raised in London when it was thought that Abdallah was about to commit himself to a long concession with APOC were, first, the question of whether Britain could have jurisdiction over foreigners living in Qatar, and second, whether it would be possible to bring the three dormant articles of the 1916 treaty into force. These were that the ruler would allow British subjects to live in Qatar and that he would undertake to protect their lives and property; that the ruler would accept a British agent to live in Qatar; and that the ruler would allow and protect the establishment of a British post office and telegraph centre.[3] Another reason for exerting new forms of pressure on Abdallah was the desire of the RAF to have regular air facilities in Qatar, and the belief that if he were closely restrained, he would grant the facilities easily.

The Political Resident, in closer touch with the realities of the situation, deprecated any moves that would only serve to antagonise the ruler, fully aware that Ibn Saud, through the machinations of Socal, was trying to absorb Qatar into Saudi Arabia. Rather than needlessly place Abdallah in a defensive position, Fowle suggested that Britain enforce Article V of the 1916 treaty, and simply tell the Shaykh that any concession had to be given to a company that was partly British. The Government of India agreed with the Resident's suggestion, adding that in order to ensure the signing of an APOC concession, the Resident should at the same time offer the protection that Abdallah had originally asked for in 1921, and the question of jurisdiction would then be a natural adjunct.[4] The India Office agreed, especially after the Resident reported that two different sources (the Air Officer Commanding in Iraq and the ruler of Kuwait) had it that Abdallah had strong relations with Ibn Saud who was warning him to desist from an APOC concession; the AOC even heard that Abdallah had gone to Riyadh with his son Hamad to sign an agreement with the King to the effect that the hinterland of Qatar, and therefore the oil in it, belonged to Saudi Arabia.[5] Once concurrence from the different departments in Whitehall had been obtained, expecially on the granting of a protection clause to Abdallah, the Political Resident felt able to go to Qatar to place all his terms before the ruler.

He arrived there on 9 March 1934 and had two meetings with Abdallah. The latter was clearly distressed at the limitations imposed on him regarding APOC, hinting that he had an agreement that ran contrary to these conditions.[6] Fowle reprimanded him for making arrangements with Ibn Saud, thus going against his treaty relations with Britain, and made it clear to him that he had to abide by the decisions made in London. The Resident left Qatar after that to give Abdallah time to think about his proposals, and returned in early April for talks that lasted three days. He found Abdallah firm about his rights; the ruler said that he would not give the concession to any company if he did not agree to the terms laid down by APOC. He also challenged Fowle's accusations that he had had no right to enter into any form of agreement with Ibn Saud, saying that this arrangement had been private and was only to keep him out of danger.[7]

A few days later, Fowle heard from a usually reliable source that Socal had offered much better terms than had the APOC.[8] Fowle thought that the ruler was now playing for time in order to have the APOC option expire in August 1934 when he would be free to negotiate with the US company.

There were other indications of the rising interest in Qatar's oil potential. Right after Ibn Saud had granted a concession to Socal, the US Government officially enquired of the British Government what the eastern frontiers of Saudi Arabia were. This was the first time the thorny question of boundaries came up officially, marking the beginning of endless debates on the subject. Although the whole question of Qatar — Saudi relations will be dealt with separately below, brief mention here will be made of the implications of the enquiry to the US Government. The enormous desert boundaries of eastern Arabia needed definition, every square mile of land now assuming great financial value. The gains, or losses, of Socal with respect to these boundaries were obviously important enough to warrant the attention of the US Government. In April 1934, the Foreign Office officially defined the eastern frontiers of Saudi Arabia as being consistent with the Blue Line (that ran due south from the head of the bay opposite Zaknuniyyah island meeting the line of demarcation between Turkish Arabia and Aden) of the 1913 Anglo-Turkish Convention.[9] Fowle was instructed to relay this statement to Abdallah with an addendum that the area between the Blue Line and the line put up by APOC was within the British sphere of influence.

Almost immediately after receiving this news, Abdallah seemed to be more disposed to APOC. Consequently, the company sent their representative, C. C. Mylles, to Qatar in July 1934, and he was able to obtain an extension of the exploratory option for eight months. But Abdallah was clearly stalling for time, and did not share Fowle's haste to 'clinch the matter'. In the meantime, to add to all the other critical factors regarding the Qatar oil concession, an official of the India Office suddenly realised that the 1916 Anglo-Qatari treaty had been made personal to Abdallah and was not binding to his heirs and successors.[10] If the ruler were to die suddenly, Britain would have to renegotiate. So there was yet one more reason to press for the finalisation of the Qatar oil concession. It was decided that once this was completed, Britain would recognise Hamad bin Abdallah as the heir to his father's position on condition that Hamad accept the obligations of the 1916 treaty.

British officials could not understand the reasons for the continued delay, and could only wonder whether Holmes was behind Abdallah's obvious reluctance to sign the agreement. They knew that Abdallah's financial situation was very unstable and that he had had to take a mortgage on his house for a debt of around 17,000 rupees.[11] They could see no other reason but Holmes's subterfuge for the ruler's intransigence. In order to be as aware as possible of the movements of rival oil companies that might seek to contact Abdallah, the local APOC agent in Doha (a merchant of Qatar, of Arab-Persian origin) was employed to secretly collect for the Political Agent in Bahrain as much information as possible for a monthly fee of 150 rupees.[12]

Abdallah, however, viewed the whole situation as a political, not a commercial, problem. He had originally refused to accept the terms of APOC for financial reasons: he wanted to be paid 500,000 rupees per annum after the first few years of the signing of the concession. The reaction to his refusal obviously surprised him. He received numerous and unprecedented visits from the Political Agent in Bahrain, even from Fowle himself. Their anxiety to put an end to the negotiations undoubtedly came across to Abdallah who, although he could never realise how important his every reaction was to a vast number of high-ranking officials of the British Empire, was aware that the oil concession held far greater implications than they were willing to admit to. Furthermore, he had the very real problem of coping with the repeated remonstrances of Ibn Saud not to sign a concession without his own approval. Despite his own impecunious state, Abdallah had no awareness of the commercial profits if the existence of oil was ever to be ascertained. For this, Mylles and Fowle were to be blamed, for in their anxiety to finalise a settlement, they deliberately played down the great wealth that Abdallah stood to gain in the event of the discovery of oil in Qatar. Thus Abdallah regarded the APOC concession as a political agreement, and wished to extract the maximum political advantages from it for himself. He understood the principle of the territorial imperative and wanted to ensure his own political stability and continuity before any financial gains could be enjoyed.

The talks between Mylles and Abdallah continued at a leisurely pace, with the latter adding new conditions, while Fowle reminded him repeatedly that APOC was the only company he was authorised to deal with. Finally, in March 1935, APOC reported that the concession was nearly ready to be drawn up. Abdallah's shrewdness and political intuition had finally won for him all he had been requesting from Britain since 1921. Fowle then had three days of meetings with the ruler in Doha in April 1935. Once all parties concerned had approved the new conditions, Fowle returned to Doha in early May to sign the agreement. Before going, however, he had decided to 'only make such of the . . . concessions [that he had already told Abdallah about] as are unavoidable and will make as much play with them as possible'.[13]

3. The Agreements

Fowle arrived in Doha on 8 May and immediately became impatient with Abdallah for wanting to check and double-check all of the Resident's promises before affixing his signature to the commercial agreement. Although this caused a delay of only two or three days, and despite his own decision to bargain with Abdallah until the last minute, Fowle was annoyed at the ruler's attitude, 'which illustrates the almost childish suspicious nature of himself and his son Hamad'.[14] Abdallah, sensing Fowle's strategy, amazed the Resident by refusing to sign the commercial agreement before actually *seeing* the money to be paid to him, not trusting a bank transfer as a substitute. Abdallah also asked for more than his annual allotment of 500 rifles, requesting machine-guns and armoured cars. The Resident wanted no further delays and petitioned the India Office to grant the request, citing the precedent of Kuwait, and asking that Abdallah be given permission to buy two armoured cars with machine guns; he added that they would, at the same time, be useful to the RAF in case of an emergency.[15] The India Office, however, refused the request on the basis of the 'lightness of the Sheikh's authority and backwardness of state'.

A formal exchange of letters between Fowle and Abdallah preceded the signing of the commercial agreement. The first, and most important to Abdallah, was the letter of protection from Fowle in the name of the British Government. Protection would be given to Abdallah on condition he signed the oil concession with APOC. The protection was to be external, i.e. against 'serious and unprovoked attacks' from outside Qatar. 'In this connection therefore His Majesty's Government naturally expect you to take all reasonable steps for your own defence and for maintaining order within your own frontier.'[16] The protection Abdallah could expect would be given to him by the RAF, which, in order to be effective, needed 'facilities' in Qatar: freedom to use wireless telegraphy, landing grounds, permission for officers to visit, and the establishment of intelligence activities.

The Resident found that he had to promise Abdallah further concessions before the ruler would sign the APOC agreement. Regarding Abdallah's request that his son Hamad be formally recognised as his heir, a letter from Fowle[17] stated that His Majesty's Government (HMG) agreed to this on condition that Hamad promise to accept the 1916 treaty on his accession. This Hamad did in writing. But Abdallah was not able to obtain any firm promises regarding British support in his internal affairs as this would run against the policy of non-interference in local matters, but HMG were 'prepared to support you and your successors in any difficulties arising from the presence of the Oil Company. In other matters which concern you the Government will not interfere.'[18] The question of jursidiction of foreigners was also settled prior to the APOC agreement. Disputes between British subjects and British-protected people and subjects of non-Muslim countries were to be settled by the Political Agent in Bahrain. After much argument, Abdallah also accepted that disputes between British subjects and subjects of non-Muslim countries and Qatari subjects were to be settled by a joint court in Doha administered by the Political Agent in Bahrain and the ruler of Qatar. But Abdallah adamantly refused to give up his rights of jurisdiction over subjects of Kuwait, Bahrain and the Trucial Coast, so Fowle allowed him this concession.[19]

Now that he had obtained a fair measure of the privileges he thought he was entitled to by the 1916 treaty — privileges he had been trying to ascertain since 1921 — Abdallah was willing to commit his signature to the APOC commercial concession. The discussions for this agreement had included Salih bin Mani, Abdallah's secretary, Hamad bin Abdallah and Yusuf Kanoo, a businessman of Bahrain and a close associate of the British representatives in the Gulf. The document was signed on 17 May 1935 for 75 years, giving APOC exclusive rights for production, transportation, refining and marketing of petroleum as well as for natural gases and other by-products. In it, the territory of Qatar was defined by a map attached to the concession, and the terms included the payment of 4 lakhs (i.e 400,000) of rupees to Abdallah on signature; with 1½ lakhs (150,000) of rupees once a year for five years followed by 3 lakhs (300,000) annually from the sixth to the seventy-fifth year.[20] If oil were to be discovered, the payments to the ruler were to be 3 rupees per ton; this figure is dramatically low, particularly when one realises that in 1935, 3 rupees were roughly equal to 4*s*. 6*d*. in the British currency of the day.

The Political Agreement between APOC and the British Government was signed on 5 June 1935.[21] Immediately afterwards, the concession was transferred to Petroleum Development (Qatar) Ltd, and Salih bin Mani and Hamad bin Abdallah were appointed the local representatives for the company. The work of the company was slow in getting under way, but by January 1938 it had employed seven Europeans, five of whom were British. It was not until October 1939 that the first slight show of oil was discovered. In January 1940, a test of the company's first well near Zekrit was reported to have been 'highly satisfactory'.

The Chief Local Representative of PC Ltd in Bahrain then suggested that the Political Agent should inform Abdallah of this, 'provided he realises that the location of one well does not necessarily constitute an oil field and royalties.'[22] By then, of course, World War II had started, and the company was forced to close operations in Qatar pending the termination of hostilities. It was not until 1949 that Qatar's large petroleum resources began to be exploited.

The rest of the story is well known. In June 1963, Petroleum Development (Qatar) Ltd became the Qatar Petroleum Company (QPC). But it was not the only oil company operating in Qatar. Although two US companies had been granted an offshore concession in 1949, it was Shell Company Qatar (SCQ), owned by Royal Dutch/Shell, that finally gained the rights to exploration. Production of oil in offshore fields began in 1964. Qatar also shares the Bunduq oil field with Abu Dhabi. It is operated by Abu Dhabi Marine Areas. In 1974, state participation reached 60 per cent in both the QPC and SCQ, and in 1976, the control of all of QPC was turned over to the Government of Qatar. Thus, just over forty years after the first concession, the wheel had turned full circle.

In the following chapter, the repercussions of the 1935 oil concession, particularly as it affected Qatar's relationship with its two closest neighbours, Saudi Arabia and Bahrain, will be examined. But it is perhaps fitting to conclude this chapter with a brief summary of how it affected Anglo-Qatari relations. The British Government became much more aware of its responsibilities towards Qatar, because of both the protection agreement and the various ramifications of the oil concession. The visits of the Political Agent in Bahrain to Doha became more frequent, as did those of the Political Resident, and gradually the sight of an Englishman in Qatar became less unusual. Friendly gestures to Abdallah were now made in order to ensure his co-operation. In June 1935, for example, Abdallah was given a medal that commemorated George V's silver jubilee because the RAF needed to undertake an aerial reconnaissance of the peninsula that same month. In November 1938, an Order-in-Council was issued to regulate the jurisdiction of foreigners in Qatar according to the terms of the 1935 exchange of letters; this was to be amended in 1949 following the independence of India. Qatar gradually began to assume the same status as the other Gulf shaykhdoms in its relationship with Britain, although it remained the most remote regarding officials, for no permanent representative in Doha existed until 1949. Abdallah, on the other hand, began to lose his earlier suspicion of British authorities. His own position in Qatar had improved a good deal. Although much of this improvement was due to his personal popularity, the existence of the protection agreement and the acknowledgement of his son as heir gave him added security and self-assurance. The long conversations with Fowle and Mylles had obviously been necessary; they proved that Abdallah's statesmanship brought the processes his father and grandfather had started to a logical conclusion.

Notes

1. The Red Line Agreement was made after a concession with Iraq in 1925 transferred the old Turkish Petroleum Company into the Iraq Petroleum Company. The participants of the new company (held in equal shares by the Anglo-Persian Oil Company, the Compagnie Française des Petroles, Shell, Standard Oil Company of New Jersey and 5 per cent for Gulbenkian) pledged not to operate within the area of the former Ottoman Empire except through the IPC.

2. S. H. Longrigg, *Oil in the Middle East* (London, 1968), p. 107.

3. L/P & S/12/3800: P. Z. 8204/33: India Office Notes on conversations with George Rendel (FO), 13 December 1933.

4. Ibid., P. Z. 493/34: Govt of India to India Office, 20 January 1934 (tele. in 4 parts).

5. Ibid., P. Z. 1703/34: Pol. Res. to India Office, 22 December 1933.

6. Ibid., P. Z. 1788/34: Pol. Res. to India Office, 24 March 1934 (tele. in 2 parts).

7. Ibid., P. Z. 2300/34: Pol. Res. to India Office, 5 April 1934 (tele. first of 2 parts).

8. Ibid., P. Z. 2473/34: Pol. Res. to India Office, 12 April 1934 (tele.).

9. J. C. Hurewitz, *Diplomacy in the Near and Middle East* (Princeton, 1956), vol. I, pp. 269-72.

10. L/P & S/12/3816: P. Z. 7118/34: Laithwaite to Walton (India Office Memorandum), 22 November 1934.

11. R/15/2/415: Pol. Agent Bahrain to Pol. Res., 15 December 1934.

12. R/15/2/924: Note by Pol. Agent Bahrain, 12 April 1934. It is interesting to note that although the Pol. Agent promised this 'secret agent' not to disclose his name to anyone and to refer to him in the files as 'K', the 'agent' gave himself away by sending his information on personalised stationery!

13. R/15/2/416: Pol. Res. to India Office, 26 April 1935 (tele.).

14. L/P & S/12/3800: P. Z. 3414/35: Pol. Res. to India Office, 12 May 1935.

15. Ibid., P. Z. 3227/35: Pol. Res. to India Office, 10 May 1935 (tele.).

16. Enclosed in Ibid., C/128.

17. Enclosed in Ibid., C/129.

18. Ibid.

19. Ibid.

20. L/P & S/18: B. 444: Qatar Oil Agreement, 17 May 1935.

21. Ibid., Memorandum B. 445.

22. R/15/2/418: Packer (Chief Local Rep., PC Ltd) to Pol. Agent in Bahrain, 13 January 1940.

7

TERRITORIAL DISPUTES: SAUDI ARABIA AND
BAHRAIN

1. Saudi Arabia

It is doubtful whether the signatories of the 1935 oil concession realised
the repercussions it was to have on Qatar's relationship with its two
closest neighbours, Saudi Arabia and Bahrain. Almost before the ink
was dry it had become imperative to mark out the uncharted desert
that linked Qatar to Saudi Arabia. Within two years, and again as a
direct consequence of the oil agreement, trouble flared up with Bahrain
regarding Abdallah's sovereignty over Zubarah; a while later, offshore
islands between Bahrain and Qatar became subjects of the same kind of
conflict.

The problems with Saudi Arabia were by far the more serious of the
two. Qatar was at a clear disadvantage from the start, its neighbour
being the more powerful of the two states. Because its treaty relations
forbade the ruler to enter into direct contact with any but the British
Government, it had to rely on Anglo-Saudi negotiations to solve its
territorial dispute. This placed Abdallah on a particularly weak footing
since any appeal to British representatives had to follow the procedure
of discussions at interdepartmental meetings in London, a time-
consuming process. Abdallah, therefore, occasionally by-passed his
treaty obligations and dealt directly with Ibn Saud or Abdallah ibn
Jaluwi, his governor in Hasa, rather than wait for help from British
sources.

During the 1920s, Abdallah had grown to fear Saudi power, for it
was then that Ibn Saud began to reap great territorial advances in the
Arabian peninsula. In 1920, he established his authority within the
borderlands of the Hijaz, and during the same year he was able to
subdue Abha, the inland part of Asir on the Red Sea coast. The next
year he finally conquered his bitter enemy, Ibn Rashid, annexing
Jabal Shammar to Nejd. In 1922, his forces pushed northwards towards
undefined boundaries and Jawf fell to him. Soon after, Ibn Saud
assumed the title of Sultan of Nejd. The final victory was in 1924
when the Wahhabis entered the Hijaz. On 13 October the holy city of
Mecca surrendered. A year later, the Hashemite dynasty in the peninsula
collapsed when Ibn Saud took Medina and Jeddah. Ibn Saud now ruled
an enormous area that extended from the Red Sea to the Gulf, from

Kuwait, Transjordan and Iraq in the north, to Yemen, Asir and the Rub al-Khali in the south. In January 1926, he became King of the Hijaz and in 1932 he was proclaimed King of Saudi Arabia.

He was now monarch over an area as large as western Europe, and had complete sovereignty and independence. Anglo-Saudi relations had to be revised: in May 1927 the Treaty of Jeddah replaced the 1915 treaty. In this agreement, Ibn Saud would only concede an assurance 'to maintain friendly and peaceful relations with . . . the Sheikhs of Qatar and the Oman Coast who are in special treaty relations with His Brittanic Majesty's Government'.[1] Ibn Saud was a pragmatist who realised the limitations of his own power, particularly in the face of British opposition. Consequently, his direct contact with Qatar as well as with the other shaykhdoms in the Gulf was remarkably limited in view of his great territorial advancement elsewhere in the peninsula. His presence in the area was very powerful, however, and constituted a constant worry to the British authorities.

We have already seen the pressure he exerted on Qatar. It was subtle and based on exploiting existing dissensions within the Al-Thani; it was also such that the British representatives could do little to combat its effects. The Political Resident remarked of the shaykhdoms of the Trucial Coast in 1930: 'We hold the front door to these principalities . . . but we do not hold the back door.'[2] The same remark, of course, applied to Qatar through whose back door the Wahhabis increased their influence. It was in the inland desert area, away from the coastal region that Britain so jealously controlled, that Ibn Saud's potency was most acutely felt. The King was a strong force in the background. But the anxious British authorities could point only once to a positive encroachment on their sphere of influence. That was in 1922 during the conference at Uqayr, when Holmes was discussing the possibility of an oil concession for Hasa with Ibn Saud. Cox was present, and he realised with a start that Ibn Saud considered all of Qatar as part of Hasa. He sharply reminded him that Qatar was outside his jurisdiction, and Ibn Saud did not press the point. When news of this reached London, a member of the Political Department of the India Office uneasily noted that 'it would have been a better sign if Ibn Saud had argued the point bitterly and fiercely.'[3]

Ibn Saud clearly did not accept it. He continued to work towards weakening Abdallah's position at home. The latter found it difficult to enforce law and order, since the Governor of Hasa invariably supported absconders, particularly members of the Al-Thani. Finally Abdallah realised that since he could not rely on British protection, he would have to reach a *modus vivendi* with his powerful neighbour. In 1930, he admitted to the Political Agent in Bahrain that he was paying Ibn Saud a secret subsidy of 100,000 rupees a year.[4] Thus, with no military effort, and only exerting subtle pressure, Ibn Saud was able to gain control of Qatar. His representatives in Hasa influenced events there, all the while giving the British Government nothing tangible to complain about. At the same time, Abdallah always maintained that he was on good personal terms with the King.

Once the APOC concession was signed, however, and with it the letters of protection, Saudi-Qatar relations entered a new phase. The main thrust of Ibn Saud's policy became the use of diplomacy as his weapon, although he also maintained personal links with Shaykh Abdallah. With both Saudi Arabia and Qatar involved in exploration for oil with two different companies, the most outstanding point became the permanent delineation of their mutual boundaries.

Two months after Abdallah signed the concession, he received a letter with a strongly worded *mulhaq* (supplement) from Ibn Saud regarding Qatar's boundaries. Here it must be noted that in the concession itself, the exact borders of Qatar were defined in an attached map that adhered to the Blue Line of 1913. From the *mulhaq* (unsealed, and attached to the formal sealed letter) it is clear that the King had not heard about the finalisation of the Qatar oil agreement; he was warning Abdallah, however, not to commit himself until the whole boundary question between them was settled. He firmly refused to accept the British suggestion of the Blue Line, and gave three reasons for this. First, the Ottomans had never exercised extensive authority or control in Hasa during their period of occupation there. Second, the King reminded Abdallah that the Anglo-Turkish Convention had been signed after he had occupied Hasa and therefore after the Ottoman occupation had ended. Finally, he referred to the fact that the Convention had never been ratified.

The *mulhaq* reveals Ibn Saud's attitude towards Qatar and the Trucial Coast, and the whole question of boundaries with them. In it, he explained to Abdallah that the British had interfered with these places, but he accepted the fact that the people of these shaykhdoms were under the formal protection of the British Government. Although he had already told British representatives that the people of Qatar and the Trucial Coast were his subjects, and that they had been the subjects of his father and grandfather before him, he accepted the fact that they themselves had chosen to be under British protection. But there was no question in his mind of their claim to anything but the towns; the desert and the allegiance of the tribes roaming that desert had always been under his sovereignty and those of his ancestors in the past. He made it clear that Abdallah had no right to claim an area he could not control or be responsible for. Regarding the Saudi-Qatar boundary, the King referred twice obliquely to an agreement already in force between himself and Abdallah, thus substantiating the latter's statement in 1930 that he was paying the King a secret subsidy in order to guarantee his own protection. Ibn Saud warned the ruler of Qatar in no uncertain terms about the consequences of signing a concession before the border problems were settled.[5] The *mulhaq* obviously disturbed Abdallah. He contacted the Political Agent in Bahrain, asking that Fowle come to Doha to discuss it. In the meantime, the ruler sent a non-committal answer to the King who was reprimanded by the British for corresponding directly with Abdallah.

However, Ibn Saud was also pursuing the border question on a different front, and on 3 April 1935, Fuad Hamza, acting Foreign Minister of Saudi Arabia, presented a proposed Saudi frontier with Qatar, the Trucial Coast, Muscat and Aden (a British Protectorate) that was to be called the Red Line or the Fuad Line. In this Line, Saudi Arabia claimed Jabal Nakhsh, the southern tip of Jabal Dukhan which lies along the west coast of Qatar; it also claimed Khawr al-Udayd. Six days later, Sir Andrew Ryan, British Minister in Jeddah, made a counter-proposal, known today as the Green Line. Since this Line was not accepted by the Saudi Government, Anglo-Saudi conversations on the Saudi frontiers took place in London in June 1935. Both sides remained firm and a deadlock ensued. In an attempt to break this deadlock, Ryan presented Ryan's Line or the Riyadh line, a modification of the Green Line, in November 1935. This gave to Saudi Arabia much of the Rub al-Khali, the great desert of central Arabia, but retained Jabal Nakhsh as being within Qatar, and Khawr al-Udayd as part of Abu Dhabi. But Ibn Saud was adamant about his claim to both Jabal Nakhsh and Khawr al-Udayd.

The tension became greater in December 1935 when Ryan learned from Fuad Hamza that sometime before 1916 Abdallah bin Qasim had written to Jaluwi, asking 'more as a favour than as a right that the King should not claim Jebel Dukhan'.[6] Apparently Ibn Saud had agreed then, but was now no longer willing to give up Dukhan. This disclosure strengthened Saudi claims, and Ryan pressed Hamza to show him proof of the request. After hesitating for some time, the Saudis finally admitted in March 1936 that the story about a letter from Abdallah to Jaluwi had been fabricated. 'What had happened was that when Ikhwan were being organised King had instructed them not to go into Dukhan or Araiq in order not to incommode Shaikh.'[7] Although the fear occasioned by Hamza's over-zealousness passed, the situation grew more critical because of the pressure of the oil companies who needed to enter the areas in dispute. Thus, in March 1937, George Rendel, head of the Eastern Department of the Foreign Office, led a delegation to Jeddah to discuss these two places with Yusuf Yasin, the Saudi Foreign Minister.[8] Once again, little progress was made. The two most important conflicts concerned Nakhsh and Udayd. On Rendel's return to London, the Foreign Office and India Office continued to discuss the issue between themselves.[9]

The Foreign Office was by now anxious to reach a compromise, aware of the growing importance of Ibn Saud as an Arab ally in the face of the deteriorating situation in Palestine, Italian activities in the Red Sea area and the growing possibilities of a war in Europe. Reader Bullard, who had replaced Ryan as British Minister to Saudi Arabia, suggested that Ibn Saud be allowed to share the profits of Jabal Nakhsh with Qatar if oil were to be discovered there. But the India Office was firm and refused to consider such a suggestion. Nakhsh was part of Dukhan, consequently an integral part of Qatar; if Ibn Saud were to be given an inch, he might take a mile, i.e. all of Qatar. Furthermore, during the nineteenth century, the Government of India had formally recognised Udayd as belonging to Abu Dhabi. The Foreign Office, presenting a divergent point of view, continued to press for a solution, convinced that the deadlock would prevail until a sizeable concession was made to Ibn Saud. The King's continuing friendship with Britain was a powerful asset in view of the general decline of British interests in the Near East. In 1937, the Cabinet agreed that a solution had to be found as soon as possible and the next year, the conclusions of a meeting of the Committee of Imperial Defence were placed before the Cabinet:

That, with a view to the settlement of the South Eastern Frontiers of Saudi Arabia on lines acceptable to Ibn Saud, the Foreign Office and India Office should be authorised to take up the question of the cession . . . by the Sheikh of Abu Dhabi of a strip of territory in the Persian Gulf known as the Khor-el-Odeid: and that, should compensation in the form of a cash payment prove necessary, the expenditure of a sum tentatively estimated at £25,000 for this purpose should be provisionally authorised, subject to the usual arrangements for obtaining Treasury sanction.[10]

By this time, there was a growing awareness that Nakhsh was in what might prove to be an important oil-producing area, and no concessions to Saudi Arabia could be made regarding Qatar's ownership; so Khawr al-Udayd was chosen instead. The India Office and the Government of India strongly opposed the CID suggestion of 'inducing' Abu Dhabi to sell or lease the Khawr; to make matters worse, the CID proposed that the British Government actually pay for the sale, around £25,000. No conclusions were reached and the whole matter was left in abeyance for much of World War II.

In 1944, the United States Government once more broached the British Government regarding specific areas of the Gulf with reference to oil exploration. The main stumbling block to a settlement at this time was the question of Jabal Nakhsh, since Khawr al-Udayd had lost its importance to Saudi Arabia which was developing Ras Tanura as a Gulf port. After the war, informal negotiations with the US Department of State regarding the Saudi frontiers in eastern Arabia took place, again with little conclusion. Throughout that time, the differences in attitude between the India Office and the Foreign Office on the question of Saudi-Qatari boundaries became greater. The former felt duty bound to protect Qatari rights, and the Foreign Office was forever conscious of the importance of Ibn Saud as an Arab ally. The Political Resident was so incensed by this attitude in 1944 that he told the Political Agent in Bahrain with exasperation that 'The Foreign Office have never been more pusillanimous towards him [Ibn Saud], and despite the fact that we are paying him three million pounds a year to do what we want, they appear to be completely mesmerised by him...'[11]

After the war, the enormous petroleum reserves of both Qatar and Saudi Arabia were beginning to be recognised and exploited. Both countries became involved in their respective economic and social development, and territorial disputes began to assume a secondary role. By 1965, the question of the Saudi-Qatar boundary was resolved amicably between the two states, and little more attention was given to the great problems of the 1930s.

2. Bahrain: Zubarah and Hawar

Qatar's relationship with Bahrain was of a totally different nature to that with Saudi Arabia. To begin with, it was the continuation of a history of conflict and antagonism between the two shaykhdoms whereas Wahhabi – Qatar relations had known long periods of friendship. The people of Qatar in general and the Al-Thani in particular had by now become strongly aware of their own separate identity and were very sensitive to any remnants of the old Bahraini suzerainty. Furthermore, the physical proximity of the two shaykhdoms and their similar economic activities, shipping and the pearl trade, added to Qatar's recent independence from Bahrain, had produced a strong feeling of resentment between the two places. Again this was unlike the relationship with Ibn Saud, which was based on the disparate size and power of Qatar and Saudi Arabia. After 1932, when oil was discovered, Bahrain became prosperous almost overnight, while Qatar continued to suffer economically from the collapse of the pearl trade. Bahrain had always been ahead of Qatar: with the help of C. Dalrymple Belgrave, the British adviser to the ruler, it had established social services, schools, hospitals and a legal system since the early part of the twentieth century; and the recent oil income served to accentuate this advance. Finally, it must be noted that any territorial claims between Bahrain and Qatar had to be resolved solely under British auspices because both places were thus bound by their respective treaty conditions, another major difference with the Saudi – Qatar dispute.

Given the above factors, it is not surprising perhaps that the persistent Al-Khalifah claim to Zubarah, the only remnant of the Bahraini claim to Qatar, should have become a major source of conflict during the years following the APOC concession. Although the ruler of Bahrain had been warned in 1875 by the Political Resident not to interfere in the affairs of Zubarah, the Al-Khalifah never accepted Qatar's ownership of the town. In 1920, Abdallah bin Isa, son of the ruler of Bahrain, had officially asked the British representative for permission to open up Zubarah as a port; the Government of India firmly refused his permission and reminded him of past remonstrances against such a possibility. It was in April 1937, however, that a visit to Zubarah by representatives of Petroleum Concessions Ltd, to make a preliminary survey for a port on the western coast of Qatar, brought the whole question of the ownership of Zubarah to a head. Needless to say, both Qatar and Bahrain claimed it and because of the recently added dimension of the presence of the oil company, the ensuing bitterness and conflict created a landmark in the modern history of Qatar. Although Zubarah had been practically deserted since the latter part of the nineteenth century, the Al-Khalifah occasionally went there on hunting trips, and the Naim tribe, whom the Al-Khalifah considered as Bahraini, grazed their flocks there, particularly during the summer months. Within a few days of the PC Ltd visit in 1937, and independently of that visit, two factions of the Naim in Zubarah had a quarrel over a woman; one of the two factions appealed to Abdallah bin Qasim in Doha. Abdallah, aware of both the interest of the oil company and that of the Al-Khalifah in Zubarah, reacted swiftly, determined to contain the Naim and establish his authority with finality. He ordered Rashid bin Muhammad, the head of the Naim at Zubarah, to swear loyalty to him or be punished, also threatening to impose a tax on the tribe. Rashid, who was a Bahraini subject and on the Bahrain civil list, appealed to Shaykh Hamad bin Isa, ruler of Bahrain. The latter sent three guards to plant the Bahrain flag on Zubarah and the Naim began to arm themselves, converging on the ruined town.[12]

As the tension mounted, the Political Resident and the Agent in Bahrain tried to contain both parties, sending for a sloop of war as a precautionary measure. The ruler of Bahrain made it clear that Zubarah was his because of the Naim tribe: its members paid no taxes to the Al-Thani and in general they obeyed the Al-Khalifah. The ruler of Qatar maintained it was an integral part of his shaykhdom. The Political Resident supported the Al-Thani claim not only because of the precedent set by the 1875 warning to the Al-Khalifah, but also because of the 1935 protection agreements he had signed with Abdallah. In order to solve the dispute on an amicable basis, he persuaded Abdallah to send a deputation to Bahrain in May 1937 for friendly talks with representatives of the Al-Khalifah. Little was accomplished, since Hamad found it difficult to relinquish his claim to Zubarah. He did agree, however, not to press for ownership of the town and his authority over the Naim on condition that Abdallah preserve the condition of Zubarah and refrain from imposing taxes on the tribe.[13] The Qatar – Bahrain talks continued for a few more weeks and then broke down completely as hostilities began.

According to Abdallah, the Naim had not kept the peace, and were being incited by Hamad, who sent them arms and provisions. In order to maintain order in Qatar, therefore, he sent a large force against them. This consisted of around 3,700 men, of whom 900 were from Doha, 2,000 from other Qatari villages and 800 from Abdallah's own guard and bedouin. The ruler issued around 800 guns and 60,000 rounds of ammunition.[14] This impressive force lost no time in inflicting a severe defeat on the Naim. Before news of the final submission to Qatar of the Naim reached Bahrain, Hamad was extremely agitated. He had been warned by the Political Resident not to interfere in the battle, and had received a letter from the ruler of Kuwait urging mediation, so he turned back his attention to ownership of Zubarah. He felt so strongly about it that he wanted to consult his London solicitors on the case. At this point, Fowle told him that it had been decided in 1875 that Zubarah belonged to Qatar and that that was the final verdict of the British Government. Hamad's bitterness increased a few days later when he learned that Rashid bin Muhammad had entered into an agreement with Abdallah, promising him the obedience of the Naim.

This final blow enraged Hamad, and a wave of anti-Qatari feeling swept his shaykhdom. He declared an embargo on trade and travel with Qatar, knowing the damaging effects it would have. All normal communications between Bahrain and Qatar broke down, and the enmity grew rather than abated with time. The Al-Khalifah found it impossible to resign themselves to the loss of Zubarah, in certain cases expressing anguish on the subject.[15] The economic boycott of Qatar was crippling in its effects, especially after the start of World War II. Bahrain, an important Gulf trade centre, had always been the market for Qatar, Doha harbour having been small and incapable of dealing with all local needs. The port and market of Dubai, considerably further away, were soon substituted at increased expense. The consequent rise in the cost of living in Qatar and the general economic slump caused a large-scale migration of Qataris to other parts of the Gulf after 1939.

Shortly after his victory, Abdallah built a new fort at Zubarah a few hundred yards next to the old one and placed guards in it. Although he did so to counteract the building of a Bahraini fort at Hawar (see below), it was like rubbing salt into the Bahraini wound and no amount of remonstrances to the Political Agent were to obtain a cessation order, for the 1875 statement was still regarded as the final British verdict. The hostility grew, and a number of minor skirmishes occurred. In 1943, the Political Agent made an attempt to solve the problem by creating a neutral zone in the Zubarah area; after some negotiations Abdallah refused to accept this solution since he regarded all of Zubarah as incontestably his.

In June 1944, another attempt was made, this time more successful. An agreement was reached and signed by both parties who accepted to restore friendly arrangements, Abdallah also promising that Zubarah would remain as it was in the past. But the presence of the new fort rankled the ruler of Bahrain, Salman bin Hamad, who had succeeded his father in 1942. It remained a constant source of humiliation, and he wanted it removed, otherwise he would sever relations with Qatar again. Throughout 1944, with the Political Agent in Bahrain as mediator, both rulers engaged in negotiations for the finalisation of the agreement with little change occurring in the *status quo*. By early 1945, the intransigence of the ruler of Bahrain had prevented any progress, for it became increasingly clear that he would always regard Zubarah as his exclusive property. The skirmishes resumed, and both parties gradually ignored the terms of the agreement.

The Political Agent in Bahrain was clearly at a loss. 'Like . . . most Political Agents, Bahrain, I get a strong feeling of nausea when the name of Zubara is mentioned.[16] The Al-Khalifah refused to relinquish their interest, which had reached the level of monomania, and Abdallah remained firm in his rights as ruler of Qatar. Further attempts by other Political Agents to reach a lasting settlement achieved little in the way of formal agreements. With time, however, the necessity for the Al-Khalifah publicly to relinquish their rights in Zubarah receded, and a gradual acceptance of the *status quo* came into being.[17] Zubarah is unquestionably part of Qatar today.

But Zubarah was not the only cause for territorial dispute between Bahrain and Qatar. The Hawar islands, which lie around 3 kilometres off the west coast of Qatar, also became the centre of controversy between the two shaykhdoms from the 1930s on. Once again, the conflict came into being as a direct result of the APOC concession. The ownership of these tiny islands had never been questioned, and the small population living there was preoccupied with fishing. In 1936, the ruler of Bahrain, aware of the new importance of territory, posted a military garrison on Hawar. Abdallah was disconcerted when, two years later, the Bahrainis began drilling for water there; the significance of any kind of underground drilling was by now well understood by every ruler in the Gulf. He complained to the Political Agent in Bahrain and said that this constituted interference in his affairs, obviously claiming the islands as part of Qatar.

In order to understand the hasty manner in which the British officials came up with a verdict on the rightful ownership of Hawar, one must bear in mind the long and drawn-out Zubarah saga; a repeat performance had to be avoided at all costs. After Abdallah's complaint, therefore, the Political Agent filed a report to the Political Resident stating that Bahrain, because of the 1936 occupation, possessed a *prima facie* claim to Hawar; Abdallah, if he wanted to claim sovereignty, had to put forward his statement of ownership for consideration.[18] Abdallah was thus put on the defensive from the beginning. He was clearly ill-equipped to present his case in the form demanded, i.e. to present a highly documented file proving his sovereignty. His correspondence with the Political Agent at the time throws much light on the attitudes of the

Arab rulers in the Gulf to the new and Western concept of territorial rights that came to the region along with the oil companies. While Belgrave, in the name of the ruler of Bahrain, presented a sophisticated treatise with photographs and the testimony of local fishermen to substantiate the Al-Khalifah claim, Abdallah, clearly bewildered, reiterated his stand. Hawar was an integral part of Qatar; everyone knew that; Bahrain had no legal rights there despite the *prima facie* claim referred to; truth and justice would prevail; and he had confidence in the fair play of the British Government.[19] In conversation with the Political Agent, who asked for factual evidence, Abdallah replied 'that he had no other evidence to offer (and saw no need for it) and that he relied on the justice of His Majesty's Government'.[20]

That answer was not good enough for Fowle who wanted to settle the case in terms of British justice. Abdallah was finally persuaded to send a folio with his claims, to which Belgrave responded with a new set of counter-claims. Bahrain presented by far the most knowledgeable case, so finally Fowle awarded the islands to Bahrain in July 1939. Abdallah refused to accept this verdict, but Fowle stood firm. C. G. Prior, who succeeded Fowle as Resident in September 1939, disagreed with his predecessor's action, convinced it had been most unfair to Qatar. 'The Hawar Islands case has been decided according to western ideas, and no allowance has been made for local custom and sentiment.' He noted that Lorimer had considered the islands as part of Qatar, and also referred to Belgrave's role in the Bahrain claim: 'Had Qatar had a British Adviser this claim could not have been made.' Prior realised, however, that it would not be 'practical politics'to reverse Fowle's decision,[21] and so the matter was laid to rest until the 1960s, when the added dimension of offshore boundaries came into play. The ruler of Qatar refused to accept an offshore settlement with Bahrain until the latter accepted Qatar's ownership of Hawar. Bahrain refused, and the negotiations came to nothing.[22] The case is still outstanding today.

Notes

1. C. U. Aitchison, *A Collection of Treaties, Engagements and Sanads Relating to India and Neighbouring Countries* (Delhi, 1933), vol. XI, p. 228. This treaty is available at pp. 227-9. Cmd. 2951 (1927).

2. L/P & S/11/222: P. 5027/22: Pol. Res. to Govt of India, 18 August 1930.

3. Ibid., P. 731/23: Minute by G. A. Simpson, 2 March 1923.

4. Ibid., P. 5875/30: Pol. Agent Bahrain to Pol. Res., 2 August 1930. Enclosed in Pol. Res. to Govt of India, 18 August 1930.

5. A copy of the *mulhaq* can be found at L/P & S/12/3848: P. Z. 6396/35: 6 Jumada I 1354/6, August 1935. Enclosed in Pol. Res. to India Office, 29 August 1935.

6. R/15/2/159: Enclosure in Ryan to FO, 10 December 1935 (copy).

7. R/15/2/160: Ryan to FO, 31 May 1936 (tele.).

8. George Rendel, *The Sword and the Olive* (London, 1957).

9. J. B. Kelly, *Eastern Arabian Frontiers* (London, 1964).

10. [PRO] CAB 23/94: 35(38)10: 27 July 1938.

11. R/15/2/465: Prior to Hickinbotham, 20 June 1944. He referred here to the wartime subsidy paid by Britain to Saudi Arabia.

12. L/P & S/12/3883: Pol. Res. to India Office, 28 April 1937 (tele.).

13. Ibid., Pol. Res. to India Office, 21 May 1937.

14. R/15/1/371. This information was compiled by a special messenger sent to Qatar for that purpose. Enclosed in Pol. Agent Bahrain to Fowle, 12 August 1937.

15. When Hamad died in 1942, C. D. Belgrave remarked that he 'remembered the words which were attributed to Queen Mary Tudor: "When I am dead . . . you shall find 'Calais' lying on my heart", but in this case the word would have been "Zabara".' C. D. Belgrave, *Personal Column* (London, 1960), p. 157.

16. R/15/2/605: Pol. Agent to Pol. Res., 23 August 1945.

17. Husain M. Al-Baharna, *The Legal Status of the Arabian Gulf States* (Manchester, 1968), pp. 248-9.

18. R/15/2/547, Pol. Agent to Pol. Res., 15 May 1938.

19. Ibid., Abdallah bin Qasim to Weightman (Pol. Agent), 10 Rabi I 1357/ 10 May 1938 and 17 Rabi I 1357/27 May 1938.

20. Ibid., Pol. Agent to Pol. Res., 3 June 1938.

21. Ibid., Prior to Peel (India Office), 26 October 1941.

22. Al-Baharna, *Legal Status*, p. 249, n. 3.

8

SOCIO-ECONOMIC FOUNDATIONS: PORTENTS FOR DEVELOPMENT

1. The Elements of a State: Qatar and the Al-Thani

The death of Shaykh Abdallah bin Qasim coincided with the beginning of the production and export of oil from Qatar. The old man had followed in the steps of his father and grandfather, governing Qatar in a fatherly fashion. The many changes in Qatar during his long reign — the 1916 treaty, the APOC concession, the British agreement, the bitter conflicts with Bahrain — were, directly and indirectly, the channels through which the shaykhdom was to begin the process of modernisation. It would be fallacious to claim today that Qatar established itself as a modern state once the income from petroleum exports enabled it to purchase modernity; it would be equally fallacious to state that it was the efforts of the three great Al-Thani rulers — Muhammad, Qasim and Abdallah — alone that made such an event possible. For it was, in fact, a combination of these two factors, the role of the Al-Thani and the oil income, that enabled the genesis and establishment of national institutions to take place.

In the preceding chapters, the gradual transformation of Qatar from a Khalifah dependency in the eighteenth century to a semi-independent shaykhdom during the first half of the present century was traced. The history of Qatar during the past two hundred years can be viewed from a number of angles. To begin with, it developed outside the mainstream of events taking place in the Gulf region and the Arabian peninsula; its position as a place of refuge, be it for the ruler of Abu Dhabi in 1820, Raqraqi the pirate in the 1830s, or the Qubaysat who turned to Khawr al-Udayd throughout the nineteenth century, gave it a special relationship with its neighbours. Above all, of course, it was its place as a base for Rahmah bin Jabir's anti-Khalifah activities that brought it into the forefront of Gulf politics in the late eighteenth and early nineteenth centuries. Its long association with Wahhabism dates from that period, as does its peculiar relationship with Bahrain.

Over the years, there emerged a number of individual leaders who, unknowingly perhaps, contributed to the establishment of the position of ruler of Qatar, and with it, the stability of the shaykhdom itself. Rahmah bin Jabir can be placed in this category, although he had no aspirations to government; the mere fact of his power, albeit directed against the Al-Khalifah, allied at different times to the Wahhabis, to Muscat and to Persia, forged the concept of an authoritative figure in the remote and isolated villages of Qatar. Although these villages were tribally constructed, each tribe having a chief, it was only when Isa bin Turayf, the chief of the Al-bin-Ali tribe, took an independent stand *vis-à-vis* the accepted relationship with Bahrain that he and his tribe began to acquire a new and different status. But the time was not propitious for the establishment of a ruling family in Qatar; although its political life was embroiled in the affairs of the Al-Khalifah and the Wahhabis, a vital element was missing. This was supplied in 1868 when Pelly went to Doha following the devastation inflicted by Bahrain and Abu Dhabi. The agreement he signed then with Muhammad bin Thani gave the latter a dimension of power that was to be upheld and reflected by his people because of the acknowledged role of Britain in the Gulf. Muhammad bin Thani had replaced Isa bin Turayf's position within the limited confines of Qatar, and it was to his advantage that the period of his ascendancy coincided with the events of 1868.

The extension of Ottoman interests in Hasa during the period following 1871 was seized by Muhammad's son as an opportunity to advance his and Qatar's position. Muhammad disagreed with Qasim's acceptance of the Ottomans, consequently retiring from his position in favour of his son, but his role in shaping the modern history of Qatar had been an essential link in the chain of events that were to lead to the independence of Qatar. Qasim's personality, like that of his father and, later, of his son Abdallah, was eminently suited to his position, and central to the development of the shaykhdom. His intuitive political abilities that played the Ottomans off against the British and that kept Abu Dhabi and Bahrain on constant alert, his strength in internal affairs and the great fortune he amassed as a pearl merchant enabled him to consolidate his power; his courage in the face of the Ottoman attack of 1891 also made him a legendary figure.

Abdallah's reluctance to succeed his father is understandable. The Al-Thani family had grown by then, and the large number of contenders who were anxious to inherit the fortunes and power of Qasim were a frightening prospect to the young man. But the astute old man had recognised Abdallah's qualities, and chose him as his heir. Abdallah got off to a weak start. The 1916 treaty was vociferously opposed by his brothers and cousins and he had to contend with their various alliances with Ibn Jaluwi while the British authorities refused to honour their agreement to help him. It was his wise handling of the negotiations for the oil concession that enabled him to strengthen his position. The protection agreements of 1935 were the logical continuation of the 1868 and 1916 agreements. They gave to Qatar the framework necessary to begin the process of modern statehood; without them, in view of the extremely limited military power of the Al-Thani, it would have been over-taken by the political forces in the Gulf and the Arabian peninsula.

The modern history of Qatar can also be regarded within the context of the ability of its people, together with its leaders, to survive in the face of gruelling economic hardship. The wave of migrations in the early eighteenth century that brought most of the present tribes of Qatar from the Arabian mainland established the main character of these people. They left the life of the desert to settle in coastal areas. Rather than build their homes around the inland water supply of Qatar, they extended this supply to the coastal regions and devoted their lives to seafaring activities, a more secure livelihood than grazing in the desert. Over the years they became skilful sailors and able fishermen, also adapting themselves to all aspects of the pearl trade. The harsh landscape did not deter the people of Qatar from gradually building coastal settlements that today have become sizeable cities. Their homes were humble enough, constructed in very rudimentary forms using all available local materials, and their diet was composed largely of the abundant fish. This ability to adapt to their environment is one of their strongest characteristics and one that has allowed the present-day citizens of Qatar to cope with the overwhelming aspects of their recent wealth.

It is highly unlikely that the people living in Doha or Wakrah during the eighteenth and nineteenth centuries were ever conscious of the concept of a Qatari nation. By the twentieth century, however, because of a variety of reasons, they began to evolve as a coherent unit; the powerful presence of the Al-Thani rulers and the continuity presented by the terms of Qatar's special treaty relations with Britain were major contributing factors. Here it must be noted that all the outward manifestations of a state that evolved in Europe – a national army, a national anthem and a flag, a strong sense of historical consciousness fostered by a national educational system – were all absent from Qatar until the very recent past. Consequently, all feelings of nationalism in the European sense of the word were absent, but a strong feeling of identity with each other existed. This was strengthened during the Bahraini blockade of Qatar and bolstered by the unusually long tenure of both Qasim and Abdallah as undisputed rulers. Although the Political Agent in Bahrain obviously exaggerated when he described the Qatari delegation to Bahrain, during the negotiations preceding the Zubarah crisis in 1937, as chauvinists, an awareness of the separateness of Qatar by then definitely existed; the quarrel over the ownership in itself is a strong indication of the new status of Qatar. This feeling, of course, was to develop enormously during the 1950s and 1960s, when Qatar began the process of building national institutions.

2. The Last Years of Abdallah: the 'Regency' of Hamad

The strong stand taken by Abdallah on Zubarah and Hawar was to be the last major contribution of his rule. He gradually handed most of his duties over to Hamad, the second of his sons, and in 1944 the Political Agent reported that Hamad even had the use of his father's seal. The insecurities of the early years of Abdallah's rule gradually declined to insignificance, although the friction with certain members of the Al-Thani family continued. After Abdallah obtained a regular income from the oil company, his relatives, who had become financially insecure with the collapse of the pearl trade and the Bahraini blockade, complained that he did not share it with them. A strong division in the ruling family resulted, with Abdallah and his sons on one side, and some of Abdallah's brothers, Abdel Aziz and Salman in particular, and his cousins, the sons of Ahmad, on the other. Of these dissatisfied people, some were content to live in penury in Qatar, occasionally complaining to the Political Agency in Bahrain, and others left Qatar and settled in Saudi Arabia. Abdallah was not unduly worried by the situation; he was by now a very popular figure in Qatar, and with the help of the 1935 protection agreement, he was no longer afraid of being displaced.

Although oil was first struck in 1939, the oil company decided in 1942 to close operations in Qatar until World War II was over. During the war years, the food supplies of Qatar, together with those of most other countries in the Near East, were under a quota system controlled by the Anglo-American Middle East Supply Centre in Cairo. Widespread discontent at the mismanagement of essential foodstuffs under this system in Qatar took the Political Agent to Doha on more than one occasion to advise Abdallah to deal fairly with the quota. With Abdallah in semi-retirement, it was at Hamad that the Political Agent directed his admonition. On closer examination he discovered that Hamad's close friend, Abdallah Darwish, was responsible for much of the unrest. He had replaced Salih bin Mani, Abdallah's secretary, as the most influential man in Qatar after the ruler and his son. Of Arab-Persian origin, Darwish was also the local agent of the Anglo-Iranian Oil Company, AIOC, as the APOC had become after 1935, a position that gave him added prestige. His older brother, Qasim, was the official *tawwash*, or pearl-buying agent, of Hamad, and together the brothers had caused widespread unrest and resentment in Qatar. Consequently, the Political Agent asked the Resident to withdraw the travelling facilities of the Darwish brothers and ask the AIOC to remove Abdallah as their agent. The Resident agreed with the former suggestion and from November 1944 to May 1946 the brothers were forbidden to leave Qatar;[1] to make the punishment official, it was broadcast over Bahrain radio. Salih bin Mani, of Nejdi origin, then returned to his former position of importance.

In the meantime, the emigration of Qataris continued. The cessation of the oil company's activities brought on even greater economic hardship, and the comparative affluence of nearby Bahrain was a major attraction. It is of course difficult to be totally accurate about the exact number of people who left Qatar at this time. But to judge from a report by the Political Agent who flew over Qatar in 1942, there were few people left in the peninsula. He even noticed a number of totally deserted villages. One could thus estimate roughly that the population, which stood at approximately 28,000 in 1939, had probably fallen to 25,000 during the years of World War II.

Hamad gradually became the *de facto* ruler of Qatar, always, however, deferring to his father's wishes. But Hamad was a sick man, suffering from a variety of ailments, including diabetes. His serious illness occasionally forced his weary father to act in his place. The old man was remarkable, and, from available accounts, it appears that he was as wise and alert in his eighties as his father had been before him. One example will serve to illustrate this point. This pertained to the decision of the Political Resident regarding the position of the Gulf states under the Bretton Woods Agreements. (The Bretton Woods meetings had been held to establish a structure for the international financial and economic system after World War II; it was there that the creation of the International Monetary Fund and the World Bank was agreed on.) Although the British Government was responsible for the Gulf states under the Agreements, the Resident was against informing the rulers of their details since 'they have no currency of their own . . . and it seems extremely unlikely that either the International Monetary Fund or the International Bank will have representation or own assets in the Shaikhdoms.' The Resident decided that the possibility of any relationship between the Agreements and the shaykdoms was extremely remote. He concluded:

For the sake of formality, I suggest that we merely inform the

Rulers that His Majesty's Government have accepted certain international obligations under the Bretton Woods Agreements, which
will have effect in their territories in all areas linked with the British
financial system. It seems preferable for our action to take the form
of an announcement rather than a request for their agreement as
the subject would be extremely difficult to explain and most of the
Rulers are unlikely to understand it despite the most detailed of
explanations.[2]

Although the Resident did just that, receiving brief acknowledge-
ments from the individual rulers, he was undoubtedly surprised by
Abdallah's answer: the ruler of Qatar was not satisfied with the announcement and replied that he wished to know more about the
Agreements.[3]

He outlived his son and heir, Hamad, who died in 1948. It was
decided soon after that Abdallah's eldest son, Ali, would succeed his
father. It has been said that at the same time Ali committed himself in
writing that Hamad's son, who was still too young to be given any
power, would succeed him. Ali was clearly his father's second choice,
never having had the innate qualities of leadership that previous Al-
Thani rulers of Qatar have displayed. He was relatively old when he
became ruler in 1949, when his father abdicated because of old age.
His contribution to Qatar in the eleven years of his rule was in no way
comparable to that of his predecessors, but by then the process of
change had set in. The oil wealth which began to pour in acted as a
catalyst for the great activity that had started to overtake the Gulf,
and Ali's character as a stabilising influence was useful at this time.
It was only when his son Ahmad succeeded him when he in turn
abdicated in 1960, thus reversing the above-mentioned decision taken
by the Al-Thani in 1948, that the differences within the ruling family
began to assume new proportions. Ahmad was ill-equipped to steer
Qatar at a time of approaching total independence. Stories of his
financial extravagance shocked even the most hardened Qatari, and
his seeming indifference to establishing a modern government, even
after the British government's decision in January 1968 to terminate
its relationship with the Gulf states in 1971, all led to his deposition.
In February 1972, Hamad's son Khalifah finally replaced him, and
remains the ruler of Qatar today.

3. The Material Base for Institutional Development: Qatar in the 1950s

Around 1943, Abdallah bin Qasim started to build the first hospital in

Qatar. The only hospitals available at the time were those of the American Mission in Kuwait, Bahrain and Muscat; they were relatively well-equipped and well-staffed, but for serious medical treatment most of the wealthy people travelled to Iraq. Although the American Mission did not build a hospital in Doha, they agreed to help Abdallah to establish one there. The ruler was motivated not only by the desire to see his ailing son Hamad receive adequate medical facilities at home; he was also anxious to introduce some urban infrastructure to Qatar, and allow his subjects to receive treatment. His resources were limited, both financially and in relation to the manpower available in Qatar. He consequently turned to the British authorities for help. He needed their assistance in the completion of the actual construction of the hospital. Although the Political Agent recommended that Abdallah be helped, the Political Resident realised that this was an opportunity to exploit the situation in order to further British political interests: he suggested that His Majesty's Government offer Abdallah the services of a doctor who could also be secretly engaged in political work for Britain;[4] this was largely because the ruler had not as yet allowed the entry to Qatar of a permanent British representative. Although nothing came of the Resident's suggestion, it is clear that the British authorities, despite their special relationship with Qatar, had no real interest in sponsoring any kind of social change there, to say nothing of initiating it themselves. The only modern school in Qatar, which had been established at Abdallah's request early in his reign, was forced to close around 1938 for financial reasons.

The material base for any kind of development was clearly lacking during Abdallah's reign. On the one hand, therefore, the lack of resources of Qatar contributed to the great perseverance and sense of survival of its people; on the other, it delayed socio-economic change. This process became unlocked after 1949 regardless of the small income that began to accrue from the sales of petroleum. The legal framework of the state of Qatar which had evolved over the past century and the characteristics of its people in the face of adversity were given the necessary impetus from what was to become a rapidly expanding sector; qualified manpower could then be imported to set the process of development into motion.

4. Socio-economic Foundations

It has all too often been said that the superimposition of Western manpower and techniques in Qatar, made possible by the income from oil, has produced a highly artificial society with basically conflicting values. Although certain aspects of contemporary Qatar might be cited to illustrate this point, the essential roots of the state naturally lend themselves to the process of development. For the traditional socio-economic foundations of Qatar have not been obstructive to the rapid transformation being undertaken today.

To begin with, the tribal loyalty of the people of Qatar, together with their acceptance of the Al-Thani for over a hundred years, have provided the necessary elements to transfer this loyalty to the state and ruler of Qatar. Although the concept of a nation is new, the underlying acceptance of such a concept has its roots firmly in the past. During the transitory phase, tribal loyalty continued to coexist with loyalty to the state; with time, however, the reality of the modern world brought home by the increasing exposure to international affairs will complete the transition.

Second, the social structure of the immediate pre-oil period was well suited for the changes about to occur. The population of Qatar was made up of bedouin, villagers and townspeople. The bedouin who belonged to Qatar proper were a relatively small number. The villagers were mainly preoccupied with fishing and petty trade, although some did join the bedouin during the winter months, going inland with their flocks. The townspeople, living mostly in Doha and Wakrah, included the major pearl merchants, the few cloth merchants and other traders; they were generally more sophisticated than their fellow Qataris and their descendants have today expanded their business interests to include contracting and heavy machinery. The learned people of Qatar also lived in Doha, as did the technicians. In 1939 roughly half the population lived in Doha, the capital city. One striking feature of Qatari society, particularly during the first half of the twentieth century, has been the large proportion of resident non-Arabs. Roughly 39 per cent of the entire population (estimated at 28,000) in 1939 were foreigners. Of these, 6,000 were negroes who had been originally slaves; rather than leave Qatar, they continued to live there, and there is no indication of discrimination against them. The number of Persians who settled in Qatar grew in the 1920s, and by 1939 there were an estimated 5,000 living in Qatar. They had originally gone there because of the pearl trade, but after its collapse they became involved in other activities. It is clear that the trouble Qasim bin Muhammad had had with the Indians was only because they were British subjects, so with the exception of one Baluchi barber, there were no Indians living in Qatar. With such a substantial non-Qatari population before oil, therefore, the large expatriate population living in Qatar today cannot be seen as a direct result of affluence but rather as the continuation of a well-established pattern.

Third, the widespread economic techniques employed in Qatar until the 1950s revolved around fishing, shipping and trade as today it revolves around the petroleum sector. Despite the financial limitations of the 1930s, and despite the fact that it was not until after World War II that shipping lines made regular calls at any port in Qatar, the preponderance of sailing craft in 1939 indicates the application of the population to their financial mainstay. In Doha alone there were 300 pearling dhows, 70 fishing boats and 40 sailing craft, the other towns and villages also having had a proportionate amount.[5] These boats were built in Qatar by carpenters from both Bahrain and Persia; thus the importation of manpower for specific purposes was not uncommon even at the height of economic hardship. Because of the limited available resources and because of their deployment for seafaring activities, roads were practically non-existent; inland transport being unmechanised, tracks were found sufficient for the purposes of the population. The rapid transformation of economic activity after 1949 also concentrated largely on the expansion of one sector, that of petroleum, although the financial ramifications have permitted a parallel diversification to include widespread social services.

The forces of change, therefore, did not rapidly disturb the social cohesiveness or mobility of the Qatari population. Although contacts with the outside world were remarkably limited, particularly during the period from 1900 to 1950 after which international communications became improved, the people of Qatar maintained regular links with Bahrain, Saudi Arabia, India and, after the Bahraini blockade, with Dubai. Doha harbour was restricted to local shipping, but most of Qatar's leading businessmen and pearl merchants went regularly to Bahrain, the most progressive and advanced of the Gulf states; they had first-hand knowledge of the European-style schools, hospitals, municipalities, police force and law courts that had been established there under the aegis of Belgrave. Qatar's relationship with India, and Bombay in particular, was also close. The entire Gulf economy was based on the Indian rupee. Furthermore, the region was largely dependent on Indian textiles for local consumption, also exporting its best pearls there. Saudi Arabia provided a different kind of contact for Qatar, many religious and intellectual leaders receiving their training in Nejd. As Dubai developed into the main entrepôt of the southern Gulf, the people of Qatar also began to form strong connections there. Arabic newspapers from Egypt, Syria and Saudi Arabia gradually began to reach Doha, and discussion of world events were not uncommon in the meeting places of the town. As a matter of fact, the people of Qatar were generally more aware of the conditions in Europe than the people in the latter place were aware of the reality of Qatar. The two articles in the English press, referred to in the Preface, best illustrate this point.

Notes

1. R/15/2/143: Pol. Agent to ruler of Qatar, 29 November 1944.
2. R/15/2/374: Prior (Pol. Res.) to Donaldson (India Office), 3 April 1946.
3. Ibid., Abdallah bin Qasim to Pol. Res., 12 Ramadan 1365/2 May 1946.
4. R/15/2/608: Pol. Res. to Govt of India, 21 December 1946.
5. L/P & S/20: C. 252, pp. 113-14.

9

ANNOUNCEMENT OF STATEHOOD

1. Federation of Emirates, 1968-70

In October 1960, a *majlis* made up of the members of the Al-Thani, together with the Political Agent in Qatar and other British representatives, met in Doha at the request of the ruler to witness his abdication in favour of his son Ahmad. Like his father before him, Ali retired because of advanced age and poor health. The Al-Thani approved of the move, declaring Ahmad the new ruler of Qatar; at the same time Hamad's son Khalifah was officially recognised as Heir Apparent and Deputy Ruler. It soon became clear that it was Khalifah as Prime Minister, rather than the ruler himself, who was going to shape an administrative system capable of carrying out the functions necessary for the development of Qatar. He assumed charge of all financial and petroleum matters, became the final arbiter in all legal cases, and was instrumental in the formulation and promulgation of laws and decrees that were issued in the name of the ruler. In short, he was responsible for government planning, policy and implementation. In 1961, for example, an *Official Gazette* was first published and, during the same year, a nationality law was laid down. Labour laws began to be issued in 1962 together with a decree to establish a labour court to settle cases regarding the application of the labour code. Other laws that laid the groundwork for the economic expansion of the 1960s included the organisation of a trade registry, the establishment of a chamber of commerce and regulations concerning foreigners engaged in trade and industry. Although no cabinets or ministries as such existed during this period, a number of important departments were created with the help of Egyptian and British advisers; these included a Lands and Registration Department, an Agricultural Department, a Customs Authority, an Immigration Service, and a Department of Labour and Social Affairs. By the late 1960s, the main legislative activities of the government were concentrated in the Departments of Legal Affairs, of Finance, of Petroleum and of Administrative Affairs.

It was during the 1960s that the large growth in the population of Qatar began to take place to meet the needs of the steadily rising economy. It is perhaps worthwhile to note here that Qatar, unlike other Gulf states, did not have a sudden and dramatic oil boom. Oil production at the start was limited, likewise, as we have seen, the income in rupees; both increased steadily throughout the following decades. Consequently, there was sufficient time for adjustment to the new modes of life to take place. Projects started on a relatively small scale at first, although it was during the 1960s that the major efforts at diversification were made. Construction of all kinds began, together with the laying down of modern roads and harbours and the building of Doha airport. The Department of Agriculture began to plant fruit trees and vegetables in hitherto intractable soil, and the diversification of industry included cement production and the harnessing of the vast fish resources into the activities of the Qatar National Fishing Company.

As the barriers between Qatar and the rest of the world began to break down, Qatar turned to the Arab world for the replacement of its old ties with Britain. The political and strategic environment of the entire Gulf region was also undergoing major changes at this time. The 1958 revolution in Iraq that overthrew the Hashemite dynasty; the 1961 independence of Kuwait that was followed by Iraqi claims to the new sovereign state; the bitter civil war in Yemen that gradually involved the forces of both Saudi Arabia and Egypt; the gathering strength of the movement of the Arab nationalists in the South Arabian Federation that resulted in widespread Anglo-Arab clashes and the hurried withdrawal of British forces; the renewal of Iranian claims to Bahrain; and the beginning of the Dhofar rebellion in Oman all had a powerful impact on the prospects for long-term stability in the region.

The effect, therefore, of the January 1968 announcement by the Labour Government in London of the termination of all British defence commitments east of Suez by the end of 1971 was particularly dramatic. In effect, this meant the termination of the old treaties of protection with the Gulf states. The pre-war hold of Britain had, of course, diminished considerably, particularly after the independence of India in 1947. British relations with the Gulf states henceforth came under the direct control of the Foreign Office in London and British officers were no longer recruited from the Indian Political Service, although the old treaties remained in force. In Qatar, the application of the dormant articles of the 1916 treaty took place in 1949 after the existence of oil resources was acknowledged; a Political Agent was appointed there together with two other Englishmen who were to serve as advisers. The British presence had constituted a maintenance of continuity in the face of the political vicissitudes of the region and the rapid transformation of its economic environment.[1] This abrupt decision to withdraw caught the Gulf states unawares.

After the initial shock had subsided, intense diplomatic activity to find an alternative to the British presence began. Qatar, like the other shaykhdoms in the Gulf, was very vulnerable; its small population and size coupled with its vast wealth and strategic location made it an obvious target for territorial expansion. After a futile attempt on the part of some of the rulers to bear the cost of a continued British military presence,[2] serious thought was given to the idea of uniting the nine Gulf states: Bahrain, Qatar, Abu Dhabi, Dubai, Sharjah, Ajman, Umm al-Qaiwain, Ras al-Khaimah and Fujairah. The first move towards unity came in February 1968 when the rulers of Abu Dhabi and Dubai announced their intention to form a federation under one flag, with joint foreign policies, defence and citizenship, inviting the other states to join. At a summit meeting of the rulers of the nine Gulf states in Dubai the same month, the Government of Qatar proposed the creation of a Federation of Arab Emirates with the establishment of a higher council to be made up of the nine rulers; this council would draw up policies regarding international relations, economics and defence. A federal council would also be created as an administrative unit to help the higher council in the formulation of policies. The Qatari proposal was accepted and at the same meeting, a declaration of union was made.

Despite Qatar's obvious conviction of the importance of such a federation, its actual creation proved to be an impossible task. As the meetings to plan for the union began, it became increasingly obvious that the obstacles were too many to be overcome easily. Differences as to when the federation should start to be implemented, how the ministries were to be distributed, where the capital was to be, who would draft the constitution, and how decisions were to be made arose from the start. Two opposing blocs within the members themselves rapidly emerged, Bahrain and Abu Dhabi on the one side, Qatar and Dubai on the other, these being the four most powerful of the nine shaykhdoms. Although Khalifah bin Hamad of Qatar was elected chairman of the Temporary Federal Council in July 1968 and the Council had a fairly successful first meeting in Doha three months later, followed by the establishment of working committees — for education, the establishment of socio-economic integration and planning, finance, postal matters, health, labour and social security, commerce, and communications — the participants remained divided on many basic issues. In their haste to react positively to the abrupt announcement of British plans, they had overlooked the enormity of the process of federalisation, the innate disparity between them and their differing motives for unity.

Bahrain, with the largest population and most advanced infra-structure, wished to play a leading role within the union; it wanted, for example, to have proportional representation in the consultative assembly that was to be established. Its main interest in the federation was to protect itself from the persistent Iranian claims which had been vigorously renewed within a short time of the British announcement of withdrawal. Qatar refused to accept Bahrain's domination of the union, feeling it had an advantageous position as the only one of the leading shaykhdoms without an imminent security problem; the amicable resolution of its border problems with Saudi Arabia had strengthened the ties between the two states, another factor that gave Qatar the edge over its prospective member states. Qatar's natural ally was Dubai, whose links with Doha had grown strong since the Bahrain blockade of the 1930s, and these had been further strengthened by the marriage of Ahmad bin Ali with the daughter of Rashid bin Said, ruler of Dubai. Furthermore, Dubai had a large Iranian population and was resentful of the strong anti-Iranian stand that Bahrain wanted all the members of the prospective union to take. Abu Dhabi, a long-time adversary of both Dubai and Qatar, was naturally aligned to Bahrain. It also had a major security problem, Saudi Arabia having recently renewed its claims to the Buraimi oasis; but its great wealth, accrued from oil revenues, offset its small population and allowed its ruler to play a prominent part in the negotiations for unity.

All in all, the nine rulers had only four meetings.[3] The first was in Dubai when the declaration of union was made. The second took place in Abu Dhabi in July 1968 when an agreement on the provisional organisation of the United Arab Emirates (UAE) was reached. The third was in May 1969, just under a year later, when the rulers met in Doha and were unable to agree on any major point. The last meeting took place in Abu Dhabi in October 1969 when Shaykh Zayid of Abu Dhabi was elected the first president and Khalifah bin Hamad the first prime minister of the federation. But no other substantial decisions were taken at this meeting. Amongst the points that resulted in a stalemate were: who the vice-president was to be; how defence was to be control-led; whether the consultative assembly was to be consultative or legis-lative, and how the different states were to be represented on it; and whether a constitution was necessary.[4] The ensuing deadlock was very discouraging to the rulers who could find no way out of the impasse.

At this point, the Political Agent in Abu Dhabi addressed the meeting, expressing his government's interest in the successful outcome of the session. For the rulers of Qatar and Ras al-Khaimah, this was the last straw; they were angered by what they regarded as British interference in their internal affairs, and walked out. The meeting thus broke up in disarray. Although the Federal Council continued to meet for some time, the federation of the nine states was virtually at an end despite efforts by Saudi Arabia, Kuwait and Britain to revive it.

In January 1970, beginning the process of independence and showing his lack of faith in the federation, Shaykh Isa bin Hamad announced the formation of the first cabinet in Bahrain; the Council of State, as it was called, was to have complete authority in internal and external affairs but had to report ultimately to the ruler. In March of the same year, there was a sudden change in Iranian policy towards Bahrain. The Shah announced that he would put the Bahrain case before the United Nations. A personal representative of U Thant, Secretary General of the General Assembly, was consequently sent there, and it was not long before the sovereignty of Bahrain was recognised by the General Assembly itself, thus putting an end to Iranian claims. It was highly predictable, therefore, that Bahrain would opt for complete independence in view of the lifting of its basic fears regarding security and the general failure of the movement towards federation.

In the meantime, and a few weeks before the UN recognition of Bahrain's independence, another event was to end the possibility of a federation of the nine emirates. This was the enactment on 2 April of a provisional constitution for Qatar, the first of its kind amongst the nine states. The constitution had been drafted by Hasan Kamil, an Egyptian who was legal adviser to the government of Qatar and who had been one of a successive number of legal experts entrusted with the drafting of a constitution for the UAE. Although the constitution referred to Qatar as being a part of the United Arab Emirates, the document itself showed little else besides this reference to confirm the statement. It frankly stated that Qatar was passing through a transitory period and that the constitution was to serve as an experimental base to determine

> the main principles governing the regulation of public authorities and of their powers, and their relations with each other, and the rights and duties of the citizens towards these authorities, *in a manner that is consonant with the actual circumstances prevailing in our country.*[5]

This was a definite move away from the idea of a federation. Although Qatar apparently sent representatives to inform the eight other states of the promulgation, this was done only 24 hours before its actual announcement,[6] giving little chance for protests. In the final analysis, Qatar had decided to go it alone. The negotiations of the fifteen previous months had achieved little in the way of progress, and, much as the idea of a federation was appealing, time was running out and some form of stability was necessary before British withdrawal.

2. The Provisional Constitution

Qatar had undergone radical change during the century since the agreement between Muhammad bin Thani and Pelly. Whereas in 1868 the Al-Thani were the chiefs of Doha, the constitution referred to Qatar as a sovereign and independent Arab state whose régime was democratic (Article 1). Qatar had passed through many stages to achieve its transformation from a cluster of coastal villages under the aegis of Bahrain to the 1970 declaration of its statehood as expressed in this new document. The bulk of these changes had been largely due to successive members of the Al-Thani family who came to rule Qatar, the Al-Thani and Qatar having been practically one and the same thing.

The provisional constitution was to alter this situation, for the functions of a government were defined as a replacement of rule by one family. This is not to imply that the Al-Thani were placed in a subsidiary position; far from it. It is rather that the people of Qatar in the 1970s were to have structured means by which they could exercise the functions of their forebears. Whereas the co-operation of the people of Qatar had been an essential factor in the maintenance of the power of the Al-Thani during the past century, this relationship had now taken on new modes to conform to the different conditions in Qatar. There is little doubt that the constitution was a direct outcome of the new economic and social order that was emerging in Qatar. Qatar had previously relied on an unwritten code which governed relationships between the ruler and his people as well as their social, political and economic behaviour. This code had been adequate before the unexpected national wealth became available, coupled with the changing political structure of the region. The constitution may have been conceived of as an instrument of independence, for it asserts the statehood of Qatar for the first time. It underlines its sovereignty by referring to the fact that it could not relinquish or cede any part of its territory or waters (Article 2), in contrast to the 1916 treaty which had bound Abdallah bin Qasim to refrain from leasing or ceding any of his territory without the approval of the British Government. Other attributes of statehood include the definition by law of the flag and national anthem (Article 3) together with that of citizenship (Article 4).

The position of the Al-Thani is confirmed in the constitution, and the fact that the ruler, the head of state, shall always be a member of this family. Khalifah bin Hamad was named Deputy Ruler and his functions as such defined.[7] Succession is referred to as being based on a consensus of notables (Article 22). In view of the importance of succession in the absence of the law of primogeniture, particularly when contrasted with other detailed items in the document, it is surprising that these notables are neither specified nor defined. It is such an omission that underlines the superimposition in the document of new and foreign concepts on the traditional forms of government. It is presumed that anyone in Qatar would know the composition of the notables, yet this is not spelled out in the constitution which supplies details on other specifications with which the people of Qatar are not as familiar.

The ruler was to be helped in his duties by a Council of Ministers, 'the highest executive organ of the State', (Article 29) and the Deputy Ruler was also to be the Prime Minister (Article 26). An oath of allegiance to be taken by the Deputy Ruler and the individual ministers is spelled out in Article 35. Ten specific ministries were to be formed within ninety days of the promulgation of the constitution: Finance and Petroleum; Education and Culture; Interior; Justice; Public Health; Public Works; Labour and Social Affairs; Industry and Agriculture; Communications and Transport; Electricity and Water (Article 33). Law no. 5 of 1970, issued by the ruler on the same day as the constitution, determined the powers of the ministers together with the functions of the ministries themselves, and an attached schedule allocated the existing government departments to the newly created ministries. Furthermore, on 24 May 1970, the ruler published his Decision no. 1, amending Article 33 to include the establishment of a Ministry of Economics and Commerce.

Another body to assist in the function of 'distributing the powers of government on a basis that is suitable to the circumstances and requirements of this experiment which is the first of its kind in the country'[8] is the Advisory Council, whose function would be to express its opinion in the form of recommendations (Article 43). The Council was to be composed of twenty elected members and the Council of Ministers plus three personal appointees of the ruler 'if he deems this necessary in the public interest' (Article 44). Despite the election of the members, the ruler was to play an important role in the formation of the Advisory Council, for 40 members (from ten electoral districts) were to be elected, and he would then choose half of them to be in the Council itself (Article 45).

Once again, an oath to be taken by the members of the Advisory Council is written out (Article 52). Thus all responsible members of the government, the Deputy Ruler, Prime Minister, Council of Ministers and Advisory Council, were to be sworn in by pledging loyalty to the state of Qatar and to the ruler; the ruler himself, however, was not bound by a similar contingency. As in the case of the notables mentioned above, one notices an internal inconsistency in the constitution. The position of ruler had evolved over a long period of time and was so generally well known on the basis of precedence that definitions of the head of state were confined to such statements as 'His person shall be accorded inviolability and it shall be a duty to respect him' (Article 20). Furthermore, the Explanatory Memorandum of the constitution makes it clear that since the ruler is elected by consensus in accordance with the procedures of the Shariah law,

it naturally follows that he should be vested with authorities and powers, and should be bound by the duties arising out of the acceptance of such election by consensus, as prescribed under Islamic Shari'a Law, which imposes a duty on those who take part in the consensus formalities, and, through them, on the whole nation, to pledge their loyalty and *absolute obedience* to the Ruler in the fear of God.[9]

This 'obedience' contradicts not only the 'respect' (Article 20) mentioned in the constitution itself, but also the spirit of the constitution which sets out to regulate and define the relationship between the government and the people. Another factor regarding the scope of authority of the ruler is the statement that he is empowered to ratify and promulgate all laws (Article 23, clause 3); at the same time, he can exercise any other power 'with which he may be vested under the law' (Article 23, clause 8). In the final analysis the ruler was entitled to revise the constitution 'by amendment, deletion or addition if he deems such revision necessary in the public interest' (Article 74). His great powers were, however, restricted to use for the public good.

It is perhaps interesting to note here a recent publication of inter-
views with Qataris, from which one gleans the impression that a con-
fusion also exists in their minds as to the difference between the state
and the ruler; the terms seem to have been used interchangeably and
at random. Furthermore, one realises that the concept of a state and/or
a government is gradually assuming realistic proportions in the minds
of the Qataris, and that many seem to equate the recent transformation
of their society with the advent of oil revenues and the rise of the
state. One person even claimed that the state came into being during
the regency of Hamad bin Abdallah.[10]

Although the organisation of the judiciary was 'to be determined by
law in accordance with the provisions of this provisional constitution'
(Article 73), the most important aspect was the *de facto* cancellation
of the Orders-in-Council in existence since 1938. Along with other
forms of independence, Qatar was to assume full charge of its justice
and 'no party whatsoever may interfere in the administration of justice'
(Article 72). All people were considered innocent until proven guilty
(Article 11) and the state promised no discrimination of race, sex or
creed in public rights (Article 9).

The constitution pledged that the state would endeavour to create
the requisite administrative organisation to ensure justice and equality
for all Qatari citizens (Article 5, clause (c)). It would also adhere to the
principles of the UN Charter regarding human rights, international
co-operation and the application of international law. But maybe more
important, it affirmed Qatar's solidarity with the Arab peoples, fully
supporting the aims of the charter of the Arab League. Since Qatar was
still a prospective member of the United Arab Emirates at the time
of the promulgation of the constitution, it pledged its positive participation in upholding the ties of unity between the member states.

The economic principles of Qatar were based on the guarantee of
the system of free enterprise (Article 6, clause (b)). Property, capital
and labour were regarded as individual rights forming basic elements
in the national social structure. Individual and collective ownership of
property were to be respected and the right of ownership could not
be removed except in the public interest (Article 16). Economic advancement through scientific planning and international co-operation was to
be a function of the state (Article 6, clause (c)).

The nucleus of Qatari society is the family, and the law would do
all it could to safeguard its unity (Article 7, clause (a)). The sanctity of
the home would be respected and guaranteed by the state (Article 12).
Islam is the religion of Qatar and the Shariah law the basis for its

legislation (Article 1). The state therefore would instil Islamic principles in society, protecting its citizens from any kind of moral disintegration. As to their physical welfare, the state pledged itself to provide everyone with medical care, both curative and preventive. The state also promised to have a plan for the social security of its citizens in cases of illness, old age or disability (Article 7).

The state declared its intention to participate in the spreading of the cultural heritage of Qatar, promoting science and the arts. (Article 8, clause (d)). For the achievement of this objective, the state would endeavour to provide education at all levels free of charge, and would implement compulsory general education. (Article 8, clause (a)). The constitution also guaranteed freedom of publication and the press (Article 13). State policy was to consolidate 'a proper basis for the establishment of true democracy, and the creation of a proper administrative organisation that will ensure justice, tranquility and equality for its citizens' (Article 5, clause (c)).

3. An Overview of Implementation

This section will concentrate on an analysis of both the traditional and new elements of the document in an effort to determine whether the articles are realistic and their application feasible. The best point from which to start is the independence and sovereignty of Qatar. A declaration of independence is the first step to the fact, and this step was taken by the promulgation of the constitution and the formal termination of the treaties with Britain which Khalifah bin Hamad announced in a television broadcast on 3 September 1971. A new Anglo-Qatari treaty of friendship and co-operation formally abrogated the old treaty, and it expressed the continuation of friendship and co-operation between the two countries. Unlike many Third World countries which obtained their independence during the 1950s and 1960s, however, Qatar did not have to pursue a long war of national liberation to achieve it. Its independence was due to a unilateral move to withdraw on the part of Britain and not the consequence of a planned policy. Furthermore, this form of independence was only second best to participation in the UAE. Bahrain's proclamation of independence left Qatar 'with no alternative but to pursue the path of independence. It was the only way to maintain and consolidate the entity of our country.'[11] Thus this first step was achieved with relatively little effort and only as an alternative to federation. But it must be pointed out that the meaning of independence was not foreign to the people of Qatar; their desire to attain some form of it is best attested by their long struggles against Bahrain during the nineteenth century. Although the 1971 declaration of independence was accomplished with relative ease, the successive steps, albeit more difficult, were not unknown to them. Whether they will be able to maintain their independence in the future, however, is still too early to predict.

The position of the ruler as laid down by the constitution is a reiteration of tradition. That he belongs to the Al-Thani, that he is the representative of the state and that his legislative and executive powers are supreme are the modern definitions of the functions of his predecessors. There is no reference to the duration of his tenure, a strong indication of the tacit reliance on past practice. Within the framework of a modern constitution, however, a conflict of interests could arise. His election by consensus and the underlying concept that he acts with the public good in mind, both rooted in history, were put to the test in the early part of 1972. By that time, Ahmad bin Ali had proved to be incapable of conforming to the new demands of his position; he had failed, for example, to establish an advisory council almost two years after the promulgation of the constitution. Furthermore, the allocation of 25 per cent of Qatar's oil revenues — estimated at between £12.5 million and £17.5 million — for his personal use contributed to the extravagance of his life-style. Acting on these and other facts that proved Ahmad's general disinterest in guiding Qatar through the changes it was undergoing, the Al-Thani family unanimously voted to replace him and chose his cousin Khalifah bin Hamad. Ahmad was abroad on 22 February 1972 when Khalifah became ruler of Qatar, a position he holds today. The deposition of Ahmad was in implicit accordance with the constitution. It was also an acknowledged reaction to the inadequacy of a ruler in the region, although it was unique to Qatar itself where Ahmad's three predecessors had abdicated because of advanced age.[12]

Another traditional aspect of the constitution is the affirmation of Islam as the religion of the state and the Shariah law as the basis for all legislation. There is no question about is applicability, particularly in view of the strong Wahhabi feelings in Qatar that are led by the Al-Thani themselves, the male members of which number roughly 500.

The creation of the instruments of government such as the Council of Ministers and the ministries themselves is a departure from tradition. It was a necessary adjunct to the independence of Qatar and the expansion of its socio-economic foundations. The actual setting up of the different organisations and the creation of government bureaucracies, while not an easy task, can be accomplished with proper advice and resources. The more difficult task to tackle is for this form of machinery to be effective in attaining the prescribed objectives; the establishment of a true democracy where all citizens are equal.

The promise of material services — education, health and welfare — for Qatari citizens is a step in the right direction. It could only have been made possible by the income from oil, but the initial mechanical stages in the establishment of a welfare system have proved the feasibility of this aspect of the constitution.

The articles regulating the foreign relations of Qatar are another departure from the past and a direct consequence of the cancellation of the treaties with Britain. Since the latter had been responsible for the conduct of all foreign relations, Qatar had to create the appropriate mechanisms to manage its new relationship with the world community, the most important of which was the Ministry of Foreign Affairs. This Ministry was not created at the time of the constitution because Qatar was still technically bound by the 1916 treaty, but the pre-existing Department of Foreign Affairs was brought into the Council of Ministers. After independence, the Ministry as such was established.

When the constitution was promulgated, it was described in the Western press as 'staggering'. Placed in the historical context of the Gulf region in general and Qatar in particular, there is little doubt that it broke new ground in more ways than one. Its proclamation of statehood at one sweep transformed Qatar from a shaykhdom into a country. The fact that it was the first of the nine Gulf states to define its functions in such detail placed Qatar in the vanguard of its neighbours. Above all, however, its claim of having a democratic régime was a remarkably bold step to take. That the constitution was provisional and of a transitory nature was presumably to prepare the grounds for a true democracy. The duality of power as expressed in the functions of the ruler described above, and as repeatedly referred to in the role to be played by the state in acting on behalf of the people for their common good, is an essential weakness of the document. But the mere fact that human rights and democracy are reiterated is a strong indication of the course Qatar has chosen for itself. Its history has been remarkably free of local opposition to the Al-Thani, a factor that might have explained its willingness to include these terms in its constitution. But by unilaterally opening up the barrier between the ruler and the people, the government of Qatar has willingly committed itself to rapid transformation and development.

4. Instruments of Government

On 1 June 1970, two months after the promulgation of the Provisional Constitution, the first cabinet (Council of Ministers) was sworn into office. The Prime Minister, Khalifah bin Hamad, was also Minister for Financial and Petroleum Affairs. Of the ten-member cabinet, seven were members of the Al-Thani. The non-Thani ministries were those of Public Works, Labour and Social Affairs, and Transport and Communications. The Ministry of Foreign Affairs was established by decree on 4 September 1971, and Shaykh Khalifah was its first Minister. When he became ruler in 1972, the position went to his brother Suhayr bin Hamad. Two other ministries have since been established; the Ministry of Interior and that of Municipal Affairs.

The functions of the council are laid down in the constitution. Besides proposing draft legislation and exercising supervision over the implementation of the laws and bills, it is responsible for the preparation of the development plans of Qatar, and thus runs the financial and administrative system of government. Each ministry has its own contribution to make towards attaining national goals, and as such is answerable to the ruler, but the council as a whole is jointly responsible politically for its performance in implementing the policy of the state. After Shaykh Khalifah became ruler, he remained Prime Minister, today serving in both functions. The discussions of the council are held *in camera*. Decisions are made on a majority basis provided a quorum has been reached. In the case of a draw, Khalifah has the casting vote. The constitution does not allow any minister to carry on any professional or commercial work while in office, and is forbidden to have any business dealings with the state. Furthermore, the ministers are appointed and dismissed by royal decree.

The council, under the leadership of Khalifah bin Hamad, is the supreme executive body of the state. The number of people in government service, estimated at 15.6 per cent of the total labour force in 1970,[13] are an indication of the wide scope of the public sector which, besides conducting the normal affairs of state, is responsible for the provision of a large number of social services in the welfare system.

The preponderance of the Al-Thani in the council is an interesting aspect of its role in the social and political life of Qatar. The very existence of the council does not in itself signify the manifestation of an intricate political system. The ministers, chosen by the ruler, are not representatives of any political parties. They do not come to the council with well-known policies, based on specific ideologies, to implement. Their first loyalty is to Shaykh Khalifah who represents the state. He is also the head of the Al-Thani family, and the majority of the council thus automatically owe him allegiance. The dual nature of a tribal society can clearly be observed here. The tribe is not only a social unit; it is also political. Its central political authority is the shaykh of the tribe, in this case the ruler. The Al-Thani being the leading family of Qatar, all other tribes also owe it their allegiance.

There are no political parties in Qatar and the people have had little or no political education except in a parochial manner. The only political authority with which they have had experience until the 1950s was the central figure of the ruler. The media, until recently, were very limited. A radio broadcasting service first began transmission in 1968, followed two years later by television broadcasts. Until 1975, there was only one daily newspaper. Because of these limitations, the political orientation of the population was slow in being developed. The existence of the council, with strong Al-Thani representation, is a step forward in the evolution of Qatar from a shaykhdom into a state. On the familiar system of tribal authority is superimposed the modern definition of government machinery. With time, the proportion of Al-Thani in the council has diminished; today, eight of the fifteen members belong to the ruling family, as compared with seven out of ten in 1970. Whether this change has come about as the result of a conscious policy or not, the fact remains that there has been a gradual shift away from the limited circle of the Al-Thani. But the ruler has to take the numerous members of his family into careful consideration, for he owes his very position to their support; without it, he could not maintain his authority. This is a vestige of the old tribal ethics that have survived until the present day, although there are indications that a change is taking place.

The Advisory Council is a definite departure from tribal political organisation. Although its functions are confined to giving recommendations, its representation covers a broad base of Qatari society. Since Ahmad bin Ali had not pursued the creation of such a council, one of the first actions of Khalifah bin Hamad as Amir was to call the council into being. This was done, and on 1 May 1972, the council was officially opened. The constitution specified that its term of office should be limited to three years; an amendment made in 1975 extended the term to six years. In 1975, membership of the council was extended by Amiri Decree from 20 to 30 people. These are expected to give their opinion on the handling of state affairs as well as to advise the government. They are also authorised to receive statements from the Council of Ministers on any domestic matter that is related to the general policy of the government. They cannot, however, interfere in the functioning of either the executive or the judiciary.

Their most important role is to approve the draft laws put forward by the Council of Ministers, for the approval of the Advisory Council is essential to the promulgation of all laws. The quorum of the Council is a majority of the total number of members, and decisions are taken on the basis of absolute majority; in the case of a draw, the President of the Council has the casting vote. Since the Council is only partly elected, and its powers rather limited, particularly in view of the fact that according to the constitution the ruler can dissolve it if the higher interests of the state are at stake (Article 68), its independence is by definition curtailed. But official pronouncements of policy have indicated that the council will have greater responsibilities in the future and that it will be given greater prominence.[14]

The judiciary, on the other hand, seems to have far more independence. The judges have a well-established authority and there are five principal courts. The higher criminal court deals with cases of major crime and the lower criminal court concerns itself with minor offences including public decency and traffic violations. The labour court deals with all cases related to work and workers. The Court of Appeal is the final arbiter on all appeals, civil and criminal. The civil court, besides its concern with civil and commercial matters, is the place to decide on all personal matters for non-Muslims. The Muslims, of course, have access to the Shariah courts.

With the establishment of a Ministry for Municipal Affairs, municipal councils under its supervision were created in Doha and other towns. These councils are made up of local residents who are entrusted with the legislative functions of municipal affairs, the actual execution being the responsibility of the government. The councils also supervise all the administrative work of the municipality including finance and the employment and dismissal of employees. In addition to the Advisory Council, they provide another opportunity for the people of Qatar to participate in the government at the grass-roots. The municipal council provides both popular representation in government and the beginnings of decentralisation of the administration.

Notes

1. This was not only political. Around 6,000 British troops were stationed at Bahrain and Sharjah.

2. See *The Times* (London), 22 January 1968, and the *New York Times*, 23 January 1968.

3. For a detailed account of these meetings, see Riyad Najib al-Rayyes, *Sira Al-Wahat wal Naft* (Beirut, 1973), Chapters 1-11.

4. Ibid., pp. 113-18.

5. Herbert J. Liebesny, 'Qatar', in A. P. Blaustein and G. H. Flanz (eds.), *Constitutions of the Countries of the World* (Dobbs Ferry, 1973), henceforth *Constitutions*), p. 1 (my emphasis).

6. Al-Rayyes, *Sira Al-Wahat wal Naft*, pp. 215-16.

7. In 1977, five years after Khalifah had become ruler, an amendment to the constitution was made, recognising his son Hamad bin Khalifah as heir apparent. Amiri Decree of 31 May 1977.

8. *Constitutions*, p. 13.

9. Ibid., p. 13 (my emphasis).

10. Helga Graham, *Arabian Time Machine* (London, 1978), p. 64, for this particular example.

11. *Speeches and Statements by HH Sheikh Khalifah bin Hamad Al-Thani* (Ministry of Information, Doha, Qatar, n.d.), speech of 3 September 1971, p. 13.

12. For an analysis of the patterns of succession in the Gulf region, see R. Said Zahlan, *The Origins of the United Arab Emirates* (London, 1978), Chapter 3.

13. See Chapter X, Table 10.3.

14. *Qatar Yearbook 1976*, p. 25.

10 SOCIAL WELFARE

Population and Manpower

No assessment of the social welfare policy in Qatar is possible without proper demographic statistics. One of the more urgent tasks of the government of Qatar is to conduct and publish a detailed official census, or preferably censuses. The 1970 enumeration has been considered largely incomplete.[1] Instead, a wide variety of estimates have been made by an equally wide selection of people and institutions; from these, it may be possible to construct a qualitative and quantitative indication of the past and present trends of the population. It must be mentioned, however, that any result is necessarily inconclusive because of the gap in official information.

The first estimate made was by Lorimer in 1908, when the figures of 26,000 to 27,000 were given; the second was made by the Government of India in 1939, with 28,000 as the figure. For the next thirty years, no indication of the number of Qataris is available, but in 1969, because of the interest evinced by the imminent independence of the shaykhdom, the general consensus seemed to put the population at 80,000. From that date to the present, a mere decade, the numbers advanced fluctuate enormously, with conflicts as large as by a factor of two. The Government of Qatar unofficially claims 202,000 or 210,000 as the population figure for 1976, and by contrast the United Nations maintains the much lower estimate of 90,000 for 1975.

Table 10.1 is a tabulation of the different official and semi-official estimates that have been made from 1908 to the present. Irrespective of the differences, one fact is abundantly clear: the population was small until the dramatic upsurge of the past twenty to thirty years. The extraordinary population growth that started during the two decades following World War II is overwhelmingly due to the influx of foreigners attracted by the opportunities of the labour market. It is probably because of this large foreign community that the government has been so reticent about the facts; the possibility that foreigners would out-number Qataris is probably seen as a destabilising factor and is therefore not officially recognised. From Table 10.1, however, it is clear that foreigners are not new to Qatar; in 1908, around 23 per cent of the population consisted of negroes who had been brought there to work in the pearl industry, and by 1939 the percentage of foreigners had risen

118

to 39 to include Iranians who had immigrated, principally to Doha, to take part in the trade. During the contemporary period, when the oil industry has replaced that of pearling, a parallel situation can be seen.

Table 10.1: Population Estimates

Year	Total	Foreign	Per Cent Foreign
1908	26,000-27,000[a]	6,000	23
1939	28,000[b]	11,000	39
1940/5	25,000[c]		
1969	80,000[d]		
1970	79,000[e]		
	80,000[f]		
	111,000[g]		59[g]
	111,100[h]		59.5[h]
	112,000[i]		
1971	90,000[j]		
	111,000[k]	65,300[k]	59[k]
1972	100,000[l]		
	126,000[m]		
1973	170,000[n]		
1975	92,000[o]		
	160,000[p]		
	170,000[q]		
1976	150,000[r]		
	180,000[s]		
	202,000[t]		
	210,000[u]		
1977	200,000[v]	150,000[w]	75[w]
			50[v]

Source:

a. J. G. Lorimer, *Gazeteer of the Persian Gulf, 'Oman and Central Arabia*, 5 vols. (Calcutta, 1908-15, republished by Gregg International, Westmead, UK, 1970), pp. 1530-1.

b. L/P & S/20: C. 252

c. Based on descriptions of local emigration from Qatar during the period of World War II when the Bahraini blockade, the depression due to the stoppage of QPC Ltd activities and the high cost of living due to the food quota system all deeply affected the population.

d. This seems to be a generally accepted estimate of 1969. Quoted by A. G. Hill, 'The Gulf States: Petroleum and Population Growth' in J. I. Clarke and W. B. Fisher (eds.), *Populations of the Middle East and North Africa: A Geographical Approach* (London, 1972), pp. 262-4. Also by 'The Union of Arab Emirates', *The Times*, 3 March 1969.

e. UN, *Singleyear Population Estimates and Projections*, ESA/P/WP. 56.
f. M. T. Sadeq and W. P. Snavely, *Bahrain, Qatar and the United Arab Emirates* (Lexington, Massachusetts, 1972), p. 15.
g. UNESOB, *UN Interdisciplinary Reconnaissance Mission, Vol. 2: Qatar*, July 1972: ESOB/D/72/23.
h. Department of Training and Career Development, Doha, *Manpower in Qatar*, 1974. Quoted in Emile A. Nakhleh, 'Labor Markets and Citizenship in Bahrayn and Qatar', *Middle East Journal* (Spring 1977) (henceforth, Nakhleh), p. 154. Figure also quoted in Ragei El Mallakh, *Qatar: Development of an Oil Economy* (London, 1979).
i. 'Qatar', *The Times*, 15 May 1972.
j. 'Independent Qatar' *Middle East Economic Digest (MEED)*, 10 December 1971, p. 1429.
k. Robert A. Mertz, *Education and Manpower in the Arabian Gulf* (American Friends of the Middle East, Washington DC, 1972), p. 115. (Henceforth, Mertz.)
l. P. Beaumont, G. H. Blake, J. Malcolm Wagstaff, *The Middle East: A Geographical Study* (London, 1976), p. 177.
m. *MEED*, Vol. 17, No. 39, 28 September 1973, p. 1131.
n. Ministry of Information (Qatar), *Qatar into the Seventies*, 1973.
o. See note (e) above.
p. 'Qatar: A Special Report', *The Times*, 23 June 1975.
q. UN/ECWA estimates, *based on ILO Yearbook of Labour Statistics* (Geneva, 1975).
r. Nakhleh, p. 154.
s. *Qatar Yearbook 1976*, p.11.
t. 'Focus on Doha', *The Times*, 2 September 1977.
u. *World Bank Atlas*, 1974.
v. Special Report, Qatar, *MEED*, London, April 1977; 'Focus on Doha', *The Times*, 2 September 1977.
w. 'Qatar', *Financial Times*, 22 February 1978.

Two types of migrants have gone to Qatar. The first, roughly equivalent to the negro slaves of the past, are the unskilled workers necessary for the heavy construction works; the lack of requisite native manpower has made the presence of these workers an essential part of the diversifying economy. The second, and here the parallel of the Iranians of the inter-war period can be cited, are the semi-skilled and skilled workers anxious to exchange their knowledge and skills for a share of the available prosperity. The two together in 1970 were officially put at 59.5 per cent of the total population of Qatar and in 1977 the estimate of their share of the population was somewhere around 64 per cent.

The foreigners in Qatar thus present only a quantitative change in the society, for there is little qualitative difference between the past and the present. In view of the fact that there was little or no destabilisation caused by the non-Qataris in the past, the portents for the future should offer none but the slightest deviation from the established trend. The total integration today of the earliest group of migrants to Qatar, the negroes, is perhaps an outstanding feature of the society. Further-more, the historical background of the main Qatari tribes and families, whereby they originally migrated to the peninsula from Nejd and Hasa in the eighteenth century, contributes to the generally absorptive capacity of the society. But the present legislation on nationality has restricted somewhat the possible integration of the new foreign community. The concern with which the government has regarded the influx of the much-needed expatriate labour led to the first nationality law which was published in 1961. Together with successive amendments, it has defined a Qatari as someone residing in Qatar before 1930. Naturalisation for Arabs is only possible after ten years of continuous residence, fifteen years for non-Arabs; even after naturalisation, native-born Qataris have first priority in employment, particularly in the public sector.

The restrictions on the acquisition of citizenship at first gave the foreign community a characteristic that is common to all those of expatriates in the Gulf states and Saudi Arabia. In view of the lack of permanence of their respective positions, the expatriates came alone to Qatar, generally leaving their families behind. Their stay there was thus unashamedly motivated by a desire to earn a profitable living and to transmit earnings abroad. With time, however, they began to send for their wives and children, and today many immigrant families are to be found in Qatar. They remain rootless, however, because of the nationality laws and are always conscious of the transitory nature of their stay in the country; this is strengthened by the law (No. 5 of 1963) that bans foreigners from owning any immovable property such as buildings or land.

Table 10.2 shows the demographic structure of the population, foreign and national, of Qatar in 1970. Two striking features can be noted immediately. The first is the swollen number (42,700) of foreigners between the ages of 20 and 59, i.e. the expatriate labour force who represent around 64.5 per cent of the total foreign community. The second fact is the large number of Qataris below fifteen years of age who alone constitute 52 per cent of the local population. It is this characteristic of Qatari society, shared by most Arab societies, that is a major contributor to the shortage of manpower. With half its population under fifteen, it is only the remaining half that is capable of being economically active. But the position of women, strictly confined by tradition, makes their contribution to the labour force extremely marginal; their participation on a whole makes for only 2 per cent, and of these the bulk are non-Qatari. Since women constitute roughly half the population, only around 25 per cent of Qataris therefore are economically active, hence the natural dependence on foreign labour, a situation exacerbated by the growing affluence.

Table 10.2: Demographic Structure of Population, Foreign and Qatari, 1970

Age in Years	Qataris	Per Cent of Population	Non-Qataris	Per Cent of Population	Total
0-5	10,500	53.8	9,000	46.2	19,500
6-14	13,000	61.8	8,200	38.7	21,200
15-19	3,900	41.9	5,400	58.1	9,300
20-59	14,300	25.1	42,700	74.9	57,000
Over 60	3,300	80.5	800	19.5	4,100
Total	45,000	40.5	66,100	59.5	111,100

Source: Department of Training and Career Development, *Manpower in Qatar* (Doha, March 1974), p. 2. Quoted in Nakhleh, p. 154.

Another by-product of the post-oil era in Qatar is the remarkable growth of Doha, the capital. In 1939, it was a town of around 12,000 people, i.e. 43 per cent of the population lived there. That figure is over 80 per cent today. The unusual concentration of people in the capital is another striking feature of Qatar. It has prompted a rapid expansion of its facilities, stretching them beyond their natural capacities and creating a strong imbalance in the rest of the country. The second largest city, Al-Khawr, is a mere 50 kilometres away, and the remainder of the labour force is concentrated at Umm Said, the industrial complex south of the capital. The majority of the Qataris have always been urban dwellers, so the present expansion is not due to rural-urban migration; it is largely due to the concentration of economic activities in the capital which has attracted the bulk of the migrant workers.

2. The Labour Force

The acute shortage of native Qatari manpower is sharpened by its inherent lack of the requisite skills for the new economy. There having been no local tradition to train youth in anything besides sailing and pearling, education having been scarce and only traditional, no professional cadres or other similar technical skills have ever existed before the contemporary expansion. While the government has acted with urgency to overcome this dearth by offering vast educational opportunities to its people, it will take some time before the gap is bridged. In the meantime, it has had to rely on foreigners for the daily working of its economy. Table 10.3 shows the economically active population, Qatari and non-Qatari, by industry. Although it is relatively dated (1970), it provides a good indication of the trends in the labour force. Two important sectors, for example, oil and construction, require little skills for the majority of the workers. Yet the Qataris have definitely shown a disinclination to work in the construction industry, leaving it almost entirely in the hands of the migrants. Their clear choice has been to work in the oil sector. It is the oldest of the new industries of Qatar, one that they have become accustomed to, and to which they have adapted. Generally speaking, work with the oil companies is less

Table 10.3: Economically Active Population by Industry and Nationality, 1970

Sector	Qataris	Per Cent	Non-Qataris	Per Cent	Total	Per Cent[a] of Total
Agriculture and fisheries	86	4.2	1,984	95.8	2,070	4.3
Manufacturing/ quarrying and public utilities	1,825	34.8	3,417	65.2	5,242	10.8
Construction	207	2.7	7,578	97.3	7,785[b]	16.1
Oil	1,259	57.0	950	43.0	2,209	4.6
Wholesale/Retail trade	880	11.2	7,005	88.8	7,885	16.1
Banking	10	3.3	292	96.7	302	0.6
Transport and communication	655	22.0	2,571	78.0	3,226	6.7
Government	1,391	22.5	4,781	77.5	6,172	12.8
Other services	1,855	13.7	11,644	86.3	13,499	27.9
Total	8,168	16.9	40,222	83.1	48,390	100.1

Note: a. This column not in above. Figures rounded, therefore do not add up to 100 per cent.
b. This figure has purportedly grown to 22,000 in 1977, 81 per cent of which is foreign. 'Focus on Doha', *The Times*, 2 September 1977. In 1974, Qatar consumed 2.4 tons of concrete *per capita* compared with 0.2 tons for Saudi Arabia, pointing to the expansion of the construction sector.
Source: Department of Training and Career Development, *Manpower in Qatar* (Doha, 19 March 1974), quoted in Nakhleh, p. 155.

gruelling than in the construction industry, particularly in view of the generous stipends received by Qataris from the state. The unskilled and semi-skilled Qataris as a whole have tended towards such jobs as those available in public utilities, transport and government, leaving those in agriculture and construction to the foreigners. In the case of banking, where Qataris would perhaps prefer to be employed, their number is still very limited because they lack the requisite technical skills.

Table 10.4 illustrates the main trends of the labour force further. The non-Qataris supply the bottom and top job scale, forming 84 per cent of the illiterates and 94.9 per cent of the most highly qualified manpower. The Qataris are strongest at the technical and primary school levels with a striking dearth of their participation at the secondary and university levels. Table 10.5 elaborates on Table 10.4 in giving the type of occupation and educational level of both Qataris and non-Qataris. The overwhelming preponderance of illiterate workers in the construction industry is striking.

Table 10.4: Economically Active Population by Education, 1970

Educational Level	Qataris	Percentage of Qataris[a,b]	Non-Qataris	Percentage of Non-Qataris[a]	Total
No education	5,100	15.8	27,200	84.2	32,300
Primary	2,200	24.7	6,700	75.3	8,900
Secondary	660	13.8	4,140	86.3	4,800
Technical	200	26.7	550	73.3	750
University	80	5.1	1,500	94.9	1,580
Total	8,240	17.1	40,090	83.0	48,330[b]

Note: a. Percentages not included in source. Figures rounded, therefore total is not exactly 100 per cent.
b. *MEED*, 'Special Report: Qatar' (April 1977), p. 3. This quotes a report by the Arab Labour Organization that 85 per cent of the total economically active population (45,000) is foreign. Qatar Government claims this figure is 68 per cent.
Source: Mertz, p. 134.

Despite the enactment of a labour law in 1962 that stated that a position must first be offered to a Qatari, then to other Arabs and finally to other foreigners, the majority of the foreigners in Qatar are non-Arabs. Although a total absence of any specific official information on the subject exists, certain basic facts are generally acknowledged. The largest single group are the Pakistanis, who in 1977 were reported by their embassy in Doha to have numbered 75,000 people.[2] Together with Indians, Omanis, Yemenis and a few Saudis, they constitute the backbone of the unskilled labour force. Another large national group, the Iranians, are said to form 23 per cent of the total population; many are descendants of the original migrants of the 1920s and are therefore well integrated. They are either merchants or in the services sector. Parallel to the Iranians in the well-defined heirarchy of expatriates are the white-collar Egyptians, Palestinians, Jordanians, Lebanese and Syrians who are employed as teachers, civil servants, doctors and engineers. At the very top are the Europeans, largely British, who, although small in number, wield considerably more influence than all other communities.

No labour unions exist in Qatar. The closest to some kind of organisation for Qatari workers are the workers committees which act as representative bodies *vis-à-vis* the oil companies and major industries.

Table 10.5: Economically Active Population by Occupation and Educational Level

| Occupation | Years of Education | | | Technical | University |
	0	1-6	6-12		
Professional, technical and related	245	295	770	380	880
Administrative and executive	60	100	245	60	275
Clerical	1,260	1,030	1,855	130	315
Sales	2,060	1,365	310	15	30
Fishing and agriculture	1,920	60	10	—	3
Transportation	3,355	960	110	10	2
Crafts and production process	15,330	2,765	1,025	135	35
Services	7,310	1,790	340	10	20
Other	760	535	135	10	20
Total	32,300	8,900	4,800	750	1,580

Source: Mertz, p. 135

Their main function has been to provide an outlet for the labour force in the major problems they face in their daily work. In 1976, there were five such committees in Qatar: for the workers in Dukhan, Umm Said, the Qatar Petroleum Company, Qatar Fertilising Company and the Shell Company of Qatar. Another institution that helps workers in any legal problems that might arise is the labour court.

But the absence of unions is not the most important factor in the labour market. The Qataris themselves have access to subsidised housing, monthly stipends in the case of needy families and other social and financial benefits that act as a built-in safety measure against any possibility of their exploitation as workers. But the immigrant worker has no such privileges and is bound by very restrictive immigration control. He is given an entry visa and a work permit only with a specific job and sponsor, and cannot change his work without the permission of his sponsor. In order to bypass these stringent regulations, many workers leave their sponsors illegally in the quest of a better or more suitable job. But the illegality of their position makes it difficult for them to claim some of the benefits to which they are entitled, thus allowing their new employers to take advantage of their vulnerability to expulsion.

3. Education

In 1951, a primary school for boys was opened in Doha with 240 students and six teachers.[3] It was not until 1956, when a Department (or Ministry) of Education was operational, however, that education on a national scale began in Qatar. That year, seventeen elementary schools for boys were started; they had a total of 1,333 students and 80 teachers. The next year, education for girls began when two schools were started with 451 students and 14 women teachers. Once the hurdle of educating girls was overcome, education for women grew at a fast rate and in 1975/6 the number of girls' schools (59) was equal to that of boys' schools. Table 10.6 shows the growth in the number of schools, students and teachers from 1956 to the academic year 1975/6.

The table indicates that great strides forward have been made. The total number of students in primary, intermediate and secondary schools in 1975/6 were almost 30,000 and the student/teacher ratio was roughly 15.6:1, an almost ideal figure; and the ratio of boys to girls, which was 2.1:1 in 1960, reached a remarkable 1.1:1 in 1975. The qualifications of the teachers in these schools are set forth in Table 10.7.

The qualifications of the teachers is another characteristic. Of the

Table 10.6: Development of Education in Qatar

Academic Year	No. of Students			No. of Teachers			No. of Schools		
	Boys	Girls	Total	Boys	Girls	Total	Boys	Girls	Total
1956/7	1,388	–	1,388	80	–	80	17	–	17
1957/8	1,879	451	2,330	105	14	119	22	2	24
1958/9	2,408	579	2,987	163	26	189	25	5	30
1959/60	3,244	1,423	4,667	286	91	377	27	11	38
1960/1	4,023	1,942	5,965	359	135	494	40	20	60
1961/2	4,607	2,450	7,057	376	144	520	46	21	67
1962/3	5,353	2,715	8,068	410	175	585	51	24	75
1963/4	6,145	3,381	9,526	419	195	614	50	27	77
1964/5	6,981	3,872	10,853	455	214	669	50	28	78
1965/6	7,906	4,811	12,717	499	237	736	49	31	80
1966/7	8,301	5,405	13,706	507	278	785	48	32	80
1967/8	8,685	5,651	14,336	525	305	830	48	34	82
1968/9	9,371	6,281	15,652	547	350	897	47	37	84
1969/70	10,122	7,101	17,223	575	381	956	48	39	87
1970/1	10,704	7,827	18,531	626	447	1,073	47	38	85
1971/2	11,883	9,096	20,979	655	510	1,165	48	41	89
1972/3	12,957	10,435	23,392	740	634	1,374	49	44	93
1973/4	13,821	11,654	25,475	813	702	1,515	51	44	95
1974/5	14,885	12,924	27,809	874	814	1,688	52	45	97
1975/6	15,855	14,087	29,942	976	950	1,926	59	59	118

Source: Ministry of Education, Doha, *Annual Report*, 1975/6, p. 47.

Table 10.7: Qualifications of Teachers

	Less than Secondary	Percentage	Secondary	Percentage	University	Percentage	Total
Primary schools[a]	41	3.5	788	67	348	29.6	1,177
Intermediate and secondary schools[b]	9	1.2	118	15.8	622	83	749
Total	50	2.6	906	47	970	50.4	1,926

Source: a. Compiled from Ministry of Education, Doha, *Annual Report*, 1975/6, p. 121
     b. Ibid.

Table 10.8: Nationality of Teachers at the Primary and Secondary Levels, 1975/6.

		Qatar	Egypt	Jordan	Palestine	Syria	Sudan	Lebanon	Saudi Arabia	Yemen and other Gulf	Other	Total
Primary:	Number[a]	444	139	260	259	24	16	6	1	20	8	1,177
	Percentage	37.7	11.8	22.2	22	2	1.3	0.5	0.1	1.7	0.7	
Secondary:	Number[b]	26	333	166	127	16	58	2	–	3	18	749
	Percentage	3.5	44.5	22.2	17	2.1	7.7	0.3	–	0.4	2.4	
		470	472	426	386	40	74	8	1	23	26	1,926
	Percentage	24.4	24.5	22.1	20	2.1	3.8	0.4	–	1.2	1.3	

Source: a. Ibid.. p. 122
b. Ibid., p. 156. Percentages not given.

intermediate and secondary school teachers, 83 per cent have a university degree and almost 30 per cent of those in primary school have attained the same level; thus, an overall average of half the entire schoolteachers have university degrees. A closer look at the nationality of the teachers (Table 10.8) reveals that Qatari teachers are in the minority. In primary schools, where teacher qualifications are lower, the Qatari teachers form 37.7 per cent of the total; in the secondary schools, where a higher level is necessary, the figure drops to 3.5 per cent. But these figures have improved during the past five years; in 1970, the corresponding figures had been 21 per cent for primary school teachers and 3.2 per cent for those in secondary schools. Thus the integration of Qataris into the educational system is taking place at a fairly rapid pace, and within the next decade, they could be expected to form the largest group of teachers. Qatar has had its own Teacher Training Institute (for men) since 1962; the equivalent for women was opened five years later. At present, the Egyptians dominate in primary and secondary teaching, followed by the Jordanians and Palestinians.

Technical education begins to be available from the intermediate and secondary levels. At the intermediate level, boys can only start either religious or industrial training. Once students have finished their intermediate schooling, they can choose between academic secondary studies (arts or sciences) or technical training. Boys have a wider choice for the latter. They can attend a school of industry, a school of commerce, a religious institute or a teachers' training institute for primary school teachers. Girls can only enter the teachers' training institute, and during the 1975/6 academic year they considerably outnumbered boys in attendance.

Other educational institutions include the private schools where only one-third of the students are Qataris; the majority are Iranian and Palestinian. Furthermore, the network of adult literacy centres and night schools provided education for over 2,000 adults in 1975. As in the case of primary and secondary education, all residents are eligible to attend, and in the case of the adult literacy classes, only one-third are Qataris, and another third are Saudis, followed by a large number of Yemenis.

At the post-secondary level, there is a Foreign Language Institute and a Management Institute. The latter is only to train government employees who have to be Qataris. There are two teacher training colleges, one for women, the other for men, which were established in 1973. They both have a number of departments and offer a Bachelor's degree. These colleges have provided the basic foundation for the new

University of Qatar which opened in 1977.[4] Finally, a Regional Training Centre in Doha to provide Qataris with sound technical and professional abilities has recently been established with the help of the UN Development Programme and the International Labour Organization; it grew out of an earlier training programme in vocational and technical skills.

In keeping with the intentions expressed in the provisional constitution, the government of Qatar has clearly embarked on a very ambitious educational programme. Education is free, and no student pays for books, transportation or equipment. Primary education is compulsory, and this will extend with time to the intermediate and secondary levels. Officially there are no distinctions between boy and girl, or man and woman teachers. But they are totally segregated, there being no mixed schools. Furthermore, girls in the secondary level do not have the wide choice of technical education that their brothers do; the only institution they can attend is the one that offers teacher training, the others being for boys only. Yet, an analysis of the results of the pupils in both the primary and secondary levels will reveal that the performance of girls has been consistently better than that of boys. The absence of women from the labour force cannot thus be ascribed to the lack of qualifications and application; given the requisite encouragement, their participation would almost certainly be a success.

Except for specific institutions, such as the intermediate and secondary level teacher training, intermediate industrial education and the Management Institute, which are restricted to Qataris, education is open to anyone living in Qatar provided he or she has the proper qualifications. The government subsidises housing in Doha for students from the villages, and scientific or cultural trips. The government also provides generous scholarships for university education abroad. During 1975/6 there were 952 students studying abroad. Of these, the majority were doing undergraduate work, but there were 40 post-graduate students studying in places as widely different as Egypt, the USA and Algeria. The greatest concentration of undergraduates was in Lebanon (213 students) and Egypt (200) with the US (53) and the UK (11) falling far behind. There seems to be no particular policy for the subjects chosen, for they vary greatly: music, history, psychology, fine arts, cinema, medicine and agriculture. In 1975/6, medicine and civil engineering attracted the largest number of students, 39 and 38 respectively.

Religious instruction plays an important role in the curriculum of students at the primary and secondary levels. At the primary level, at least 20 per cent of the total teaching hours are devoted to this subject. In the early years of educational expansion, Qatar had to rely on imported textbooks from Jordan and Egypt; it now has a programme to write and produce its own textbooks. A most striking feature of the attitude towards education is revealed by an examination of the amount allotted to it in the annual budget. In 1975, 120 million riyals were allocated to education; the next year, the figure grew to 200 million and in 1977, it was to have reached 800 million. This last jump reflects the concentration on the building and operating of the new university.

From the foregoing description of the varied aspects of education in Qatar, there can be no doubt of the great advancement made, particularly during the past ten years. The results as set forth above have been impressive. Qatar has implemented most of the provisions spelled out in Law No. 5 of 1970 to establish the functions of the Ministry of Education. But the spirit of these provisions – 'To sponsor and preserve the national cultural heritage and assist in spreading it' and 'To promote and guarantee education as a means to expand culture and as the pillar of progress' – cannot be ascertained or measured easily. Two features are necessary before these goals can be attained. The first is the full participation of women in Qatari society. Although girls are being given generally equal opportunities in education and although they have already proved their superior abilities, they have not yet been supplied with the proper motivation for entering the labour market. In view of the large foreign population in Qatar, a full integration of Qatari citizens is necessary in order to preserve the national heritage. This would be difficult to achieve without the participation of the whole population in the move towards progress. As the situation stands today, half the population is immobilised because of the constraints placed on women. Furthermore, according to the principle of the constitution, all citizens are equal, irrespective of religion or sex. This gives to women an equal opportunity to make their contribution to the social, cultural and economic development of Qatar.

Second, while the quantification of the educational system stands well to the test, the building of the future society of Qatar cannot be measured in the same way. At present, the characteristics of Qatari society lie in the contradictions between the maintenance of tradition and the reality of the space age. Qatar is eager to maintain links with both these forces, the past and the present. The best way to safeguard tradition is to imbibe the students with an acute sense of social and historic consciousness. This cannot be done by the traditional methods of education where learning by rote is the main step towards qualification. It is only when a vision of the future is clarified in the minds of the educators that it can be imparted to the youth. This entails a continuous examination and re-examination of Qatar's place in history, past and present.

Notes

1. United Nations Economic Commission for Western Asia (ECWA), *Demographic and Related Socio-economic Data Sheets for Countries of the ECWA* (Beirut, 1978).

2. See 'Focus on Doha', *The Times*, 2 September 1977.

3. Mahmud Bahjat Sinan, *Tarikh Qatar al-Am* (Baghdad, 1966), p. 177.

4. For further information on this project, see UNESCO, *Future Development of the University of Qatar* (January 1978) (FMR/ED/SC/78/209 (FIT)).

11 PROSPECTS FOR THE FUTURE: YEAR 2000

1. What is the Future?

In developed countries there is considerable concern about the future. The motivations are many, and range from an imaginative curiosity to a desire to be better prepared for the unknown. Generally speaking, there are two major trends of thought. In the first, the futurologists are interested in the impact of science and technology on the human race; the problems they tackle include artificial intelligence, biological engineering and genetic surgery, eternal life and eternal youth on earth and communication with other intelligent beings in distant planets.[1] In the second, the futurologists are more down-to-earth and their anxiety is about the immediate future; they are concerned about population explosions, mineral resources and fossil fuel reserves, pollution, orbital colonies, news management and mind control. Here one finds the analysts worrying about nuclear warfare, state control, freedom of the individual in the emerging computerised societies, the future of the nation state and the balance of power between the superpowers. Futurologists in this category vary from prophets of doom to harbingers of utopias.[2]

Analysts, scholars and speculators residing in stable and large societies are firmly based in highly articulated cultures. They attempt to project the possible consequences of complex new ideas, of facts and events. Scientific discoveries and technological breakthroughs hold an important place in these speculations. Well-established technical achievements, such as optical communication systems and nuclear reactors, are the concerns of planners and rarely attract the attention of the avant-garde futurologist.

Qatar is one of the smallest states in the UN family of nations. The problems of futurology do not trouble its leaders, and neither science nor technology finds a prominent place in its institutions. Yet the future evokes anxieties far more pressing than either genetic surgery or the population explosion. During the past two decades, the rapidly increasing income generated from oil exports has brought new possibilities and opportunities to the people and government of Qatar. Because of this, the events and issues under consideration here are neither dire events that will arise from the exhaustion of natural resources nor the blissful consequences of the acquisition of eternal youth. They are rather the

134

projection of current processes that are visible and fairly comprehensible.

The tiny community of Qatar has been — and will continue to be — assured of a substantial income by a number of major oil and gas companies. Despite the numerous existing voices of doom regarding the impending depletion of oil reserves, it must be noted here that Qatar enjoys considerable unassociated gas reserves that have not yet been tapped. With this income, the government of Qatar has embarked at high speed on a very ambitious programme to provide widespread social services and virtually unlimited access to the opportunities and comforts of Western technology. These include air travel, air-conditioners, electronics, advanced medical services, water, electricity and even sandwiches flown in daily from the UK for schoolchildren. Qataris travel widely today, they own property in the major capitals of the world; they even send their children to study at Eton, Harrow and Harvard. Practically every Qatari has been exposed to a totally new life-style, to new possibilities and opportunities.

Thus the 'future' of Qatar is being formed and moulded at this very moment. The fact that one can find in Qatar today both a former slave and a woman physicist[3] is indicative of the creative response to changing circumstances and of the rate at which changes occur. The future is not contingent on technological breakthroughs, but rather on a fairly limited and precise set of forces and constraints. In societies where change has been occurring in a stable fashion, it is normal to expect that the future will be an extension of the past. Projections attenuated by various likely technological, social and political developments constitute the methodology for forecasting a future condition and for constructing likely scenarios. Such a situation does not prevail in Qatar. Instead, the construction of likely futures will have to be based on an identification of the forces at work and on the analysis of their interactions within the field of possibilities now available.

2. The Inner and Outer Limits

In Qatar, the 'inner limit' set by social cohesiveness and the replacement of old social values with new viable ones is closer than the 'outer limit' set by the radical change of external forces. It is assumed that the major external force that will continue to bear on Qatar will be that of Saudi Arabia. The two countries share a common border, both are Wahhabi, and in recent years they have enjoyed a close relationship. It seems likely that, barring the unexpected, these conditions will endure. It also seems probable that Qatar will develop its relationship with other neighbours and become party to future moves for closer forms of a Gulf federation.

Therefore the outer limits — finance and external relations — will remain essentially the same.

The dynamics of change will thus be essentially governed by the evolution of internal forces stimulated by the recent affluence. The critical role played by a small number of powerful men in the shaping of the history of Qatar has been amply emphasised in the preceding chapters. Until recently, the role of the individual Qatari was subdued by poverty and the lack of means, and restricted by the ties of powerful tribal bonds. Today, however, the new opportunities presenting themselves to young Qataris with a university education are considerable and will increase with time as new banks are created, as more businesses expand and as professional careers become more prevalent. The demand for doctors, teachers, bankers, engineers and traders will continue to increase; this plus the lure of the concomitant Western life-styles will combine to weaken the cohesive forces that have in the past sustained Qatari society.

Most important of these are the tribal bonds. The emerging bureaucracy of Qatar today is a hybrid of the old tribal world and the new world of management and job descriptions. Foreign firms and consultants advise, design plants, contract projects and operate oilfields and hospitals. The emerging Qatari youth are gradually becoming eligible for these jobs, fewer and fewer of which will be dependent on tribal affiliations, and more and more on technical expertise. The critical shortage of Qatari manpower and the existing norms, however, militate against the development of standards of excellence and rigorous work ethics; both are vital elements in an actively changing society. Their future existence would depend on the absorption of women into the labour force and the normalisation of the position of expatriates. Naturally, tribal affiliations will never be dissolved entirely, for the strains of the modern jet age act to draw people together as a refuge from the buffeting they receive elsewhere.

Furthermore, the traditional power base is being expanded. We have already noted, for example, the growing number of cabinet ministers from outside the Al-Thani. On the socio-economic level, the prominent merchants of yesterday, such as the Darwish and the Mani, are still predominant today; this fact, however, does not preclude the entry into big business of newcomers.

Although Qatari women may be lagging behind their Egyptian or Lebanese counterparts, they are already infinitely better off than they were a mere decade ago. The growing number of educated women that has given rise to a group, albeit small, of professional women — doctors, teachers, scientists — has started to pave the way towards the acceptance of women as equal members of society. The gradual emancipation of women will sooner or later challenge all the basic precepts of male chauvinism, particularly in a society as small as Qatar, where every added member to the economically active population is obviously desirable.

The direction clearly points to the partial replacement of the extended family by the nuclear family. As the Qataris continue to be educated, to travel abroad, to have professional women and to be exposed to Western values and life-styles, their family units will shrink and become more self-contained.[4] As with tribal relations, it is unlikely that the extended family will disappear entirely; to revert to the strength and warmth of family ties will always be a welcome relief from the strains of modern life.

The changing values and structure of society will, by and large, serve to advance the position of the individual. Freed from the shackles of poverty, and with ample educational opportunities behind him, he will play a much more important role in the development of his country. The position of the ruler and government will obviously need to grow correspondingly. The latent tension between a tribally constituted power structure and the proclaimed democratic society as defined in the constitution has already been noted. How this tension will be resolved will bear directly on the quality of life. The past rulers of Qatar have played an instrumental role in culling out a firm place for the tiny shaykhdom. Courage, political shrewdness, tenacity and a bit of luck were some of the qualities that enabled the Al-Thani shaykhs to escape Bahraini rule, Ottoman power, Saudi hegemony and British gunboats. Today these qualities would be insufficient. The state of Qatar faces no immediate threats from without or within. But the changing structure of its society calls for measures of a cultural, social and intellectual nature. The need to replace the old order with a new and viable one that is consistent with the social and economic circumstances of Qatar is at least as great a challenge as any a Qatari ruler has had to face. There are indications that the present ruler is aware of the new trends. He has taken a number of steps that underline this awareness, the most outstanding being his declaration of action upon assuming power in 1972: he then increased public salaries, cancelled outstanding loans for housing, and reduced the ruler's salary by a considerable amount.

3. The Possible Routes to Economic Well-Being

The likely futures of Qatar are obviously determined by the present natural and financial resources. Because of its size, Qatar, like all other similar nations, will never be self-sufficient in the sense of producing all its needs. To sustain the present level of its economy it must be integrated in, or at least transact with, larger economic systems. At the moment Qatar's interaction with external economies is narrow-based and restricted to a few commodities. It is a common policy of all the oil-producing countries to attempt to diversify their economies and to prepare for the depletion of their oil and gas reserves. In Qatar the possibilities for diversification lie in two directions: trade and finance; and industry. In both cases the activity has to be 'export' oriented and in both cases the activities may be distributed between the regional, Arab and international spheres.

It must be noted that the economic problems Qatar must prepare to face are unlike those faced by most other nations of the world. For with a reasonable degree of careful financial management and shrewd investments of current revenue, Qatar will be assured of ample means in the year 2000. Thus, it is more relevant to speculate about the likelihood of Qataris pressing forward their comparative advantages to create for themselves enduring activities that would at the same time consolidate their social cohesiveness and establish constructive functions internationally and within the Arab world.

The traditions of the Gulf communities in international commerce and finance are deeply rooted in history. The flowering seen during the ninth to the fourteenth centuries was curtailed with difficulty by the different European powers, particularly the Portuguese and the British. The successful trading experience of Dubai in the modern pre-oil era has proved that these traditions were never stifled entirely. Since independence, all Gulf states have exhibited a wide diversity of interests in the banking and trading sectors. The continuous appearance and/or acceptance of new schemes is indicative of the aptitudes and possibilities that lie ahead.

The numerous bilateral and multilateral arrangements being entered into by the different Gulf states, on the private and public levels, within and outside the Arab world, point to the emerging scope and style of commercial and financial activities. Some of the projects undertaken may have been ill-advised and/or politically motivated. But Qatar, along with the other Gulf states, is becoming increasingly involved in large-scale trade, banking, finance and investments in long-term schemes of regional, Arab and international importance. Investments in the development of Sudanese agriculture, in the Arab Petroleum Investments Corporation, in the Arab Maritime Petroleum Transport Company and numerous other activities related to investment in downstream operations in the distribution and processing of petroleum in Europe are examples of this trend.

Qatar's participation is not restricted to the supply of capital. More and more Qataris are assuming key positions in national, regional and international institutions and committees. Thus the process of exploring new functions and roles is well under way.

Since the nineteenth century, Third World countries have viewed industrialisation as the route to economic prosperity. Whereas only Japan was successful in making the transition from a feudal to an industrial state, many a Third World country has attempted to do the same. As the oil-producing countries became aware of the limits of their oil reserves, some adopted the policy that energy and capital-intensive industries should be established to generate future income once the oil reserves run down. Many of these industries were initially designed to utilise flared gases as an alternative to the export of liquefied methane and ethane. It may very well be that the Qatari share in the capital of a project is small and it is rather the supply of gas at low cost that constitutes the significant contribution to these projects. This gas may have been flared and its industrial use is not a loss. We are not concerned here with whether an industrial plant in Qatar is economically profitable to a foreign firm. From the viewpoint of Qatar the question is whether the erection of industrial plants will in itself generate income and/or employment commensurate with need once oil and gas exports decline; also whether the Qataris will be able to acquire the necessary technological and managerial skills to husband these resources and investments.

5. Conclusion

It is clear from the above that although Qatar has the financial means essentially to retire and live from the proceeds of current investments, both the government and the private sector have opted for the pressing forward of their advantages. We have already pointed out that tribal bonds have to be superseded, that new relationships between the people and the government are called for and being formed, and that an era of exploration of new roles is well under way. Of course the challenges are many and the stakes high. For example, the current industrial strategy faces many problems, in both the tiny Gulf states and in the larger developing countries.

The fact that every bit of the industry has to be designed and manufactured abroad, imported, installed and operated by foreign manpower whose housing, food and entertainment also have to be imported has increased the cost of industrial installations.[5] According to field studies by the Industrial Development Centre of Arab States (IDCAS), the peformance of Arab petrochemical plants, with few exceptions, has been far from satisfactory.[6] In the iron and steel industry the experience of the Arab states is also disquieting: the unit cost per ton of steel is a few times greater than production cost in advanced countries.[7]

Most of the industries being established in Qatar are export-oriented, thus resulting in a high sensitivity to the conditions of world trade. Qatar has wisely attempted to associate itself with foreign investors and industries who could guarantee the satisfactory operations of the plant and the marketing of its products. Nevertheless, the absence of a national expertise in science and technology leaves the country and its investments totally dependent on foreign advice. The full range of contingencies that affects the worthiness of these investments cannot be fully appreciated. Furthermore, and equally important, the limited industrial base of a small state renders it sensitive to industrial accidents. For example, the major fire at the Umm Said NGL plant in April 1977 had serious psychological as well as industrial repercussions.

Although industry has several appealing features, it appears at the moment doubtful whether a continuation of present patterns will lead Qatar to its ultimate goal of economic viability, although a judicious modification of current policies could overcome some of the outstanding difficulties.

The trading and finance alternative, however, is much more viable. The key factors for the successful establishment of such a sector — capital and manpower — already exist. It should not be difficult in a short time to adequately train a requisite number of people in the intricacies of banking, transportation, insurance and trade; this cadre need not be as heavily foreign as it would be in industry. Furthermore, in view of the local traditions established during the past centuries, including the well-defined systems of the pearling industry, the adjustment of the society as a whole would be kept to a minimum. Here the recent successful example of Bahrain as a financial centre can be cited; with much less capital than Qatar, it has drawn on the wealth of the accumulated experiences of the past to develop a banking capability. Steps in the right direction have already been taken by the creation of banks and trading companies in Qatar. Given the proper legal framework, the sector could expand to open new horizons for the people of Qatar.

During the eight years since independence the government and people of Qatar have expanded their social and economic activities and engaged themselves in the creation of a large variety of new institutions. Regardless of whether the industrial or banking alternative — or both, or none — is chosen, the fact remains that all these socio-economic activities have so far been independent enclaves, isolated from each other, each one the product of the initiative of a handful of persons. This disjointedness is detrimental to national development. At the moment there exists an impressive set of disconnected units ranging in scope and quality from a power generator to a university. The Qatar of the future will depend to a large extent on the degree to which these innovations are integrated and fused with the country's national heritage in order that it may be passed on to the generations to come.

Notes

1. Gerald Feinberg, *The Prometheus Project* (New York, 1969); Gordon Rattray Taylor, *The Biological Time Bomb* (New York, 1969).

2. Donella H. Meadows, Dennis L. Meadows, Jørgen Randers and William W. Behrens III, *The Limits to Growth* (New York, 1972); Mihajlo Mesarovic and Eduard Pestel, *Mankind at the Turning Point* (New York, 1974); Herman Kahn, William Brown and Leon Martel, *The Next 200 Years: A Scenario for America and the World* (New York, 1976); Amilcar O. Herrera *et al.*, *Catastrophe or New Society, A Latin American World Model* (Ottawa, 1976); A. B. Zahlan, *Arab World: Year 2000* (Beirut, 1975).

3. See the section on Zalikha, the former slave, and on the wife of Mohammad, Director of the Electricity Department, in Helga Graham, *Arabian Time Machine* (London, 1978), pp.119-20 ff. and p.162 ff.

4. Evidence of the start of this trend is given in the case of the woman physicist studying for her PhD in Cairo while her husband remains in Doha to look after their house and four children. Graham, *Arabian Time Machine*, pp.119-20.

5. Michael Field, 'Perils for Oil States' Industrial Life-rafts', *Financial Times*, 17 April 1978.

6. 'Arab Co-operation in the Development of the Arab Chemical Fertilizer Industry', an IDCAS Working Paper presented to the Second Meeting of The Arab Ministers of Industry, Tunis, 8-13 November 1977.

7. Omar Grine, 'Transfer of Technology in the Arab Steel Industry' in A. B. Zahlan (ed.), *Technology Transfer and Change in the Arab World* (Oxford, 1978).

APPENDIX I: THE AL-THANI FAMILY: GENEALOGICAL TABLE

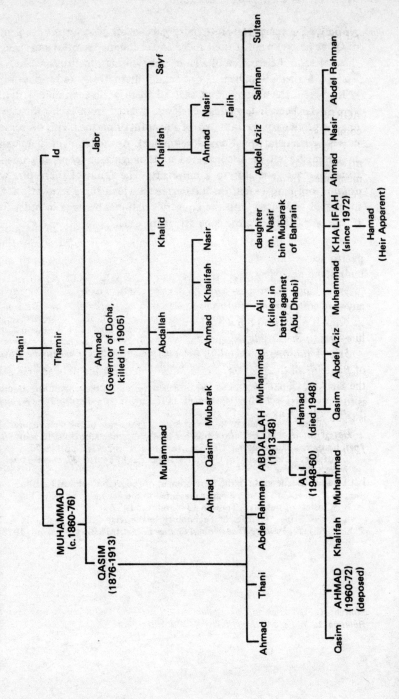

APPENDIX II: THE 1868 TREATY

AGREEMENT of the CHIEF of EL-KUTR *(Guttur)* engaging not to commit any BREACH of the MARITIME PEACE,–1868.

I, MAHOMED BIN SANEE, of Guttur, do hereby solemnly bind myself in the presence of the Lord, to carry into effect the undermentioned terms agreed upon between me and Lieutenant-Colonel Pelly, Her Britannic Majesty's Political Resident, Persian Gulf:–

1st.–I promise to return to Dawka and reside peaceably in that port.

2nd.–I promise that on no pretence whatsoever will I at any time put to sea with hostile intention, and in the event of disputes or misunderstanding arising, will invariably refer to the Resident.

3rd.–I promise on no account to aid Mahomed bin Khalifeh, or in any way connect myself with him.

4th.–If Mahomed bin Khalifeh fall into my hands, I promise to hand him over to the Resident.

5th.–I promise to maintain towards Shaikh Ali bin Khalifeh, Chief of Bahrein, all the relations which heretofore subsisted between me and the Shaikh of Bahrein, and in the event of a difference of opinion arising as to any question, whether money payment or other matter, ;the same is to be referred to the Resident.

Dated on the 24th of Jemadi-ool-awul 1285, corresponding with the 12th of September 1868.

Scaled in our presence by Mahomed bin Sanee of Guttur, on this the 12th day of September 1868.

LEWIS PELLY, *Lieut.-Col.,*
H. B. M.'s Poltl. Resdt., Persian Gulf.

R. A. BROWN, *Capt.,*
Comdg. H. M.'s Ship "Vigilant".

Source: C. U. Aitchison, *A Collection of Treaties, Engagements and Sanads Relating to India and Neighbouring Countries* (Delhi, 1933), vol. XI, p. 255.

APPENDIX III: THE 1916 TREATY

TREATY between the BRITISH GOVERNMENT and the SHAIKH of QATAR,–1916.

Treaty between the British Government and Shaikh 'Abdullah bin Jasim bin Thani, Shaikh of Qatar, dated the 3rd November 1916.

Whereas my grandfather, the late Shaikh Mohammed bin Thani, signed an agreement on the 12th September 1868 engaging not to commit any breach of the Maritime Peace, and whereas these obligations to the British Government have developed on me his successor in Qatar.

I.

I, Shaikh 'Abdullah bin Jasim bin Thani, undertake that I will, as do the friendly Arab Shaikhs of Abu Dhabi, Dibai, Shargah, Ajman, Ras-ul-Khaima and Umm-al-Qawain, co-operate with the High British Government in the suppression of the slave trade and piracy and generally in the maintenance of the Maritime Peace.

To this end, Lieutenant-Colonel Sir Percy Cox, Political Resident in the Persian Gulf, has favoured me with the Treaties and Engagements, entered into between the Shaikhs abovementioned and the High British Government, and I hereby declare that I will abide by the spirit and obligations of the aforesaid Treaties and Engagements.

II.

On the other hand, the British Government undertakes that I and my subjects and my and their vessels shall receive all the immunities, privileges and advantages that are conferred on the friendly Shaikhs, their subjects and their vessels. In token whereof, Sir Percy Cox has affixed his signature with the date thereof to each and every one of the aforesaid Treaties and Engagements in the copy granted to me and I have also affixed my signature and seal with the date thereof to each and every one of the aforesaid Treaties and Engagements, in two other printed copies of the same Treaties and Engagements, that it may not be hidden.

III.

And in particular, I, Shaikh Abdullah, have further published a

144

proclamation forbidding the import and sale of arms into my territories and port of Qatar; and in consideration of the undertaking into which I now enter, the British Government on its part agrees to grant me facilities to purchase and import, from the Muscat Arms Warehouse or such other place as the British Government may approve, for my personal use, and for the arming of my dependents, such arms and ammunition as I may reasonably need and apply for in such fashion as may be arranged hereafter through the Political Agent, Bahrein. I undertake absolutely that arms and ammunition thus supplied to me shall under no circumstances be re-exported from my territories or sold to the public, but shall be reserved solely for supplying the needs of my tribesmen and dependents whom I have to arm for the maintenance of order in my territories and the protection of my Frontiers. In my opinion the amount of my yearly* requirements will be up to five hundred weapons.

IV.

I, Shaikh 'Abdullah, further undertake that I will not have relations nor correspond with, nor receive the agent of, any other Power without the consent of the High British Government; neither will I, without such consent, cede to any other Power or its subjects, land either on lease, sale, transfer, gift, or in any other way whatsoever.

V.

I also declare that, without the consent of the High British Government, I will not grant pearl-fishery concessions, or any other monopolies, concessions, or cable landing rights, to anyone whomsoever.

VI.

The Customs dues on the goods of British merchants imported to Qatar shall not exceed those levied from my own subjects on their goods and shall in no case exceed five per cent. *ad valorem*. British goods shall be liable to the payment of no other dues or taxes of any kind whatsoever, beyond that already specified.

VII.

I, Shaikh 'Abdullah, further, in particular, undertake to allow British subjects to reside in Qatar for trade and to protect their lives and property.

*NOTE.—In the original Treaty in the English version the word "early" has been written for "yearly" by slip of the pen (Aitchison's note).

VIII.

I also undertake to receive, should the British Government deem it advisable, an Agent from the British Government, who shall remain at Al Bidaa for the transaction of such business as the British Government may have with me and to watch over the interests of British traders residing at my ports or visiting them upon their lawful occasions.

IX.

Further, I undertake to allow the establishment of a British Post Office and a Telegraph installation anywhere in my territory whenever the British Government should hereafter desire them. I also undertake to protect them when established.

X.

On their part, the High British Government, in consideration of these Treaties and Engagements that I have entered into with them, protect me and my subjects and territory from all aggression by sea and to do their utmost to exact reparation for all injuries that I, or my subjects, may suffer when proceeding to sea upon our lawful occasions.

XI.

They also undertake to grant me good offices, should I or my subjects be assailed by land within the territories of Qatar. It is, however, thoroughly understood that this obligation rests upon the British Government only in the event of such aggression whether by land or sea, being unprovoked by any act or aggression on the part of myself or my subjects against others.

In token whereof I, Lieutenant-Colonel Sir Percy Cox, Political Resident in the Persian Gulf, and I, Shaikh 'Abdullah bin Jasim bin Thani, have respectively signed and affixed our seal to this original document and four copies, thereof.

Dated 6th Moharram 1335, corresponding to 3rd November 1916.

'ABDULLAH BIN JASIM,
Chief of Qatar.

P. Z. COX, *Major General,*
Political Resident in the Persian Gulf

CHELMSFORD,
Viceroy and Governor-General of India.

This treaty was ratified by the Viceroy and Governor-General of India in Council at Delhi on the 23rd day of March A.D. one thousand nine hundred and eighteen.

A. H. GRANT,
Secretary to the Government of India,
Foreign and Political Department.

Source: Aitchison, *Collection of Treaties*, pp. 258-61.

BIBLIOGRAPHY

1. India Office Records

L/P & S/5: Secret Correspondence with India, 1756-1874
L/P & S/6: Political Correspondence with India, 1792-1874
L/P & S/7: Political and Secret Correspondence with India, 1875-1911
L/P & S/10: Departmental Papers: Political and Secret Separate (or Subject) Files, 1902-31
L/P & S/11: Departmental Papers: Political and Secret Annual Files, 1912-30
L/P & S/12: Departmental Papers: Political External Files and Collections, *c*. 1931-50
L/P & S/20: Political and Secret Library
V/23   Selections from the Records of the Government of India
R/15:   Persian Gulf Territories, Residency Records
   R/15/1: Bushire, Political Residency, 1763-1948.
   R/15/2: Bahrain Political Agency, 1899-1950.

2. Public Record Office (PRO)

F.O. 371: Eastern Affairs
C.A.B.:   Cabinet Conclusions

3. Official Publications

(A)   Britain

Aitchison, C. U.
   A Collection of Treaties, Engagements and Sanads,
   vol. XI. Delhi, 1933

Great Britain: Admiralty (Naval Intelligence Division). *Iraq and the Persian Gulf*. London, 1944

Great Britain: HMSO. *The Persian Gulf Pilot*. London (seventh edition), 1924

Lorimer, J. G.
   Gazeteer of the Persian Gulf, 'Oman and Central Arabia, 2 vols. Calcutta, 1908-15. Republished by Gregg International, Westmead, UK, 1970

(B) League of Arab States

'Arab Co-operation in the Development of the Arab Chemical Fertilizer Industry', An IDCAS Working Paper presented to the Second Meeting of Arab Ministries of Industry, Tunis, 8-13 November 1977

(C) Qatar

Frank O'Shanohun Assoc. Ltd (for Government of Qatar). *Qatar 1968*. Essex, 1968

Ministry of Economy and Commerce. *An Economic Survey of Qatar, 1969-1973.* Doha, 1974

Ministry of Education. *Annual Report 1975/76.* Doha

Ministry of Information. *Qatar into the Seventies.* 1973

Ministry of Information. *Speeches and Statements by H.H. Sheikh Khalifah bin Hamad Al-Thani.* Doha, n.d.

Ministry of Labour and Social Affairs. *Annual Report, 1974/75.* Doha, 1975

Ministry of Labour and Social Affairs. *Annual Report, 1975/1976.* Doha, 1976

Qatar Yearbook 1976

(D) United Nations Organisations

ILO Yearbook of Labour Statistics, 1975 UN Economic Commission for Western Asia (ECWA). *Demographic and Related Socio-Economic Data Sheets for Countries of the ECWA.* Beirut, 1978

UNESOB. *UN Interdisciplinary Reconnaissance Mission, vol. 2, Qatar.* July, 1972 (ESOB/D/72/23)

UNESCO. *Future Development of the University of Qatar.* January, 1978 (FMR/ED/SC/78/209/(FIT))

UNESCO. *Qatar, An Educational and Socio-Economic Study.* March 1974.

World Bank Atlas, 1974

4. Arabic Publications

al-Aqqad, Salah. *al-Istmar fil-Khalij al Farisi.* Cairo, 1956

al-Aqqad, Salah. *al-Tayyarat al-Siyasiyyah fil-Khalij al-Arabi.* Cairo, 1965

al-Dawud, Mahmud Ali. *al-Khalij al-Arabi wal-Alaqat al-Duwaliyyah, 1890-1914.* Cairo, 1963

Hamzah, Fuad. *al-Bilad al-Arabiyyah al-Saudiyyah.* Mecca, 1937

Hamzah, Fuad. *Qalb Jazirat al-Arab.* Cairo, 1933

Nawfal, al-Sayyid Muhammad Ali. *al-Awda al-Siyasiyyah li Imarat al-Khalij al-Arabi.* Cairo, 1960

Qasim, Jamal Zakariyya. *al Khalij al-Arabi, 1914-1945.* Cairo, 1973

Rayyes, Riyad Najib. *Sira al-Wahat wal-Naft* Beirut, 1973

Rida, Adil. *Uman wal Khalij.* Cairo, 1969

Rihani, Ameen. *Muluk al-Arab.* Beirut, 1925

Rihani, Ameen. *Tarikh Najd wa Mulhaqatihi.* Beirut, 1972 (new edition)

al-Salimi, Muhammad, bin Abdallah and Naji Assaf. *Tarikh. . . Yatakallam.* Damascus, 1963

al-Shaybani, Muhammad Sharif. *Imarat Qatar al-Arabiyyah bayn al Madi wal-Hadir.* Beirut, 1962

Saqr, Abdel Badi, *Dalil Qatar al-Jughrafi,* n.p., n.d.

Sinan, Mahmud Bahjat. *Tarikh Qatar al-Am.* Baghdad, 1966

al-Siyabi, Salim bin Hamud. *Isaf al-Ayan fi Ansab Ahl Uman.* Beirut, 1965

al-Takriti, Salim Taha. *al-Sira ala al-Khalij al-Arabi.* Baghdad, 1966

Wahbah, Hafiz. *Jazirat al-Arab fil-Qarn al-Ishrin.* Cairo, 1967

5. European Publications

(A) Books

Abir, Mordechai. *Oil, Power and Politics: Conflict in Arabia, the Red Sea and the Gulf.* London, 1974

Adamiyat, Fereydoun. *Bahrain Islands.* New York, 1955

Anthony, John Duke. *Arab States of the Lower Gulf: People, Politics, Petroleum.* Washington, DC, 1975

Aramco. *Oman and the Southern Shore of the Persian Gulf.* Cairo, 1952

Arberry, A. J. (ed.). *Religion in the Middle East,* vol.2. Cambridge, 1969

Armstrong, H. C. *Lord of Arabia.* Beirut, 1966

Avery, Peter. *Modern Iran.* London, 1965

al-Baharana, Husain M. *The Legal Status of the Arabian Gulf States.* Manchester, 1968

Beaumont, P., Blake, G. H., Wagstaff, J. M. *The Middle East: A Geographical Study.* London, 1976

Belgrave, Sir Charles Dalyrymple. *Personal Column.* London, 1960

Benoist-Mechin. *Le Loup et le Léopard, Ibn Séoud.* Paris, 1955

Berreby, J. J. *Le Golfe Persique.* Paris, 1959

Blaudstein, A. P. and Flanz, G. H. (eds.). *Constitutions of the Countries of the World.* Dobbs Ferry, 1973

Bullard, Sir Reader. *Britain and the Middle East.* London, 1951

Bullard, Sir Reader. *The Camels Must Go: An Autobiography.* London, 1961

Busch, Briton C. *Britain and the Persian Gulf, 1894-1914.* Berkeley, California, 1967

Busch, Briton C. *Britain, India and the Arabs, 1914-1921.* Berkeley, California, 1971

Caroe, Olaf. *Wells of Power.* London, 1951

Chisholm, Archibald H. T. *The First Kuwait Oil Concessions Agreement: A Record of the Negotiations, 1911-1934.* London, 1975

Clarke, J. I., Fisher, W. B. (eds.). *Populations of the Middle East and North Africa: A Geographical Approach.* London, 1972

Coen, Terence Greaph. *The Indian Political Service.* London, 1971

Dickson, H. R. P. *The Arab of the Desert.* London, 1967

Feinberg, Gerald. *The Prometheus Project.* New York, 1969

Fenelon, K. G. *The United Arab Emirates.* London, 1973

Finnie, David H. *Desert Enterprise.* Cambridge, Mass., 1958

Fowle, Capt. T. C. *Travels in the Middle East.* London, 1916

Graham, Helga. *Arabian Time Machine: Self Portrait of an Oil State.* London, 1978

Graves, Philip. *The Life of Sir Percy Cox.* London, 1941

Guilmartin, John Francis Jr. *Gunpowder and Galleys: Changing Technology and Mediterranean Warfare at Sea in the Sixteenth Century.* London, 1974

Harrison, Paul W. *Doctor in Arabia.* London, 1943

Hay, Sir Rupert. *The Persian Gulf States.* Washington, DC., 1959

Herrera, Amilcar O. *et al. Catastrophe or New Society: A Latin American Model.* Ottawa, 1976

Hopwood, Derek (ed.). *The Arabian Peninsula: Society and Politics.* London, 1972

Humaidan, Ali. *Les Princes de l'Or Noir, Evolution Politique du Golfe Persique.* Paris, 1968

Hurewitz, J. C. *Diplomacy in the Near and Middle East,* 2 vols. Princeton, 1956

Issawi, Charles. *An Arab Philosophy of History,* London, 1950

Kahn, H., Brown, W., Martel, L. *The Next 200 Years: A Scenario for America and the World.* New York, 1976

Kelly, J. B. *Britain and the Persian Gulf, 1795-1880.* Oxford, 1968

Kelly, J. B. *Eastern Arabian Frontiers.* London, 1964

Kumar, Ravinder. *India and the Persian Gulf: 1858-1907, A Study of British Imperial Policy.* New York, 1965

Longrigg, Stephen H. *Oil in the Middle East*. London, 1968

Low, C. R. *A History of the Indian Navy, 1615-1863*. London, 1877

Mallakh, Ragei el. *Qatar: Development of an Oil Economy*. London, 1979

Marlowe, John. *The Persian Gulf in the Twentieth Century*. New York, 1962

Meadows, D. H., *et al. The Limits to Growth*. New York, 1972

Mertz, Robert Anton. *Education and Manpower in the Arabian Gulf*. AFME Gulf Study, Washington DC, 1972

Mesarovic, Mihajb and Pestel, Eduard. *Mankind at the Turning Point*. New York, 1974

Mikdashi, Z. M., Cleland, S., Seymour, I. (eds.). *Continuity and Change in the World Oil Industry*. Beirut, 1970

Miles, S. B. *The Countries and Tribes of the Persian Gulf*. London, 1966 (reprint)

Mineau, Wayne. *The Go-Devils*. London, 1958

Monroe, Elizabeth. *Britain's Moment in the Middle East, 1914-1956*. London, 1965

Monroe, Elizabeth. *The Changing Balance of Power in the Persian Gulf*. American Universities Field Staff, New York, 1972

Nicholls, C. S. *The Swahili Coast*. London, 1971

Palgrave, W. G. *Personal Narrative of a Year's Journey through Central and Eastern Arabia*. London, 1877

Philby, II. St. J. B. *Arabian Oil Ventures*, Washington DC, 1964

Ramazani, Rouhallah K. *The Persian Gulf: Iran's Role*. Virginia, 1972

Rendel, Sir George W. *The Sword and the Olive*. London, 1957

Rihani, Ameen. *Around the Coasts of Arabia*. London, 1930

Rihani, Ameen. *Ibn Saoud of Arabia*. London, 1928

Sadeq, M. T. and Snavely, W. P. *Bahrain, Qatar and the United Arab Emirates*. Lexington, Mass., 1972

Sanger, Richard H. *The Arabian Peninsula*. Ithaca, New York, 1954

Shwadran, Benjamin. *The Middle East, Oil and the Great Powers*. New York, 1959

Stanford Research Institute. *Area Handbook for the Peripheral States of the Arabian Peninsula*. Washington DC, 1971

Taylor, Gordon Rattray. *The Biological Time Bomb*. New York, 1969

Troeller, Gary. *The Birth of Saudi Arabia: Britain and the Rise of the House of Saud*. London, 1976

Twitchell, K. S. *Saudi Arabia*. Princeton, 1958

Vadala, R. *Le Golfe Persique*. Paris, 1920

Vidal, F. S. *The Oasis of al-Hasa*. New York, 1955

Wilson, Lt. Col. Sir Arnold T. *The Persian Gulf*. Oxford, 1928
Winder, R. Bayley. *Saudi Arabia in the Nineteenth Century*. New York, 1965
Woodruff, Phillip. *The Men who Ruled India: The Guardians*. London, 1954
Zahlan, A. B. *Arab World: Year 2000*. Beirut, 1975
Zahlan, A. B. (ed.). *Technology Transfer and Change in the Arab World*. Oxford, 1978
Zahlan, Rosemarie Said, *The Origins of the United Arab Emirates*, London, 1978

(B) Articles

Al-Rumaihi, Mohammad. 'The 1938 Reform Movement in Kuwait, Bahrain and Dubai' (in Arabic), *Journal of the Gulf and Arabian Peninsula Studies*, Vol. 1, No.4 (1975)
Belgrave, Sir Charles Dalyrymple. 'Pearl Diving in Bahrain', *Journal of the Royal Central Asian Society*, Vol. XXI (1934)
Belgrave, Sir Charles Dalyrymple. 'Persian Gulf — Past and Present', *Journal of the Royal Central Asian Society*, Vol. LV (1968)
Bentley, G. W. 'The Development of the Air Route in the Persian Gulf', *Journal of the Royal Central Asian Society*, Vol. XX (1933)
Berreby, Jean-Jacques. 'Progres et Evolution des Principautés Arabes du Golfe Persique', *Orient*. No. 25 (1963)
Birks, J. S. and Sinclair, C. A. 'International Migration Project. Case Study: Qatar', University of Durham, Dept. of Economics (February, 1978)
Bowen, Richard Le B., Jr. 'Marine Industries of Eastern Arabia', *Geographical Review*, Vol. XLI (1951)
Bowen, Richard Le B., Jr. 'Pearl Fisheries of the Persian Gulf', *Middle East Journal*, Vol. V (Spring 1951)
Burchall, Col. H. D. S. O. 'The Political Aspect of Commerical Air Routes', *Journal of the Royal Central Asian Society*, Vol. XX (1933)
Cox, Sir Percy Z. 'Some Gulf Memories' (reprinted from *The Times of India Annual*) (1928)
Dalyell of the Binns, Lt.-Col. G. 'The Persian Gulf', *Journal of the Royal Central Asian Society*, Vol. XXV (1938)
Harrison, P. W. 'Economic and Social Conditions in East Arabia', *Muslim World*, Vol. XIV (1924)
Haworth, Col. Sir Lionel. 'Persia and the Persian Gulf', *Journal of the Central Asian Society*, Vol. XVI (1929)

Hay, Sir Rupert. 'The Impact of the Oil Industry on the Persian Gulf Sheikhdoms', *Middle East Journal*, Vol. IX (1955)

Hay, Sir Rupert. 'The Persian Gulf States and their Boundary Problems', *Geographical Journal*, Vol. CXX (1954)

Heard-Bey, Frauke. 'The Gulf States and Oman in Transition', *Asian Affairs*, Vol. LIX (new series, Vol. 111) (1972)

Holden, David. 'The Persian Gulf after the British Raj', *Foreign Affairs*, Vol. 49, No.4 (July 1971)

Jong, Garett de. 'Slavery in Arabia', *Muslim World*, Vol. 33 (1934)

Kumar, Ravinder. 'The Dismemberment of Oman and British Policy Towards the Persian Gulf', *Islamic Culture*, Vol. 36 (1962)

Liebesny, Herbert J. 'Administration and Legal Development in Arabia: the Persian Gulf Principalities', *Middle East Journal* (X, 1956)

Liebesny, Herbert J. 'British Jurisdiction in the States of the Persian Gulf', *Middle East Journal* (III, 1949)

Liebesny, Herbert J. 'The International Relations of Arabia: The Dependent Areas', *Middle East Journal* (I, 1947)

Lindt, Dr A. R. 'Politics in the Persian Gulf', *Journal of the Royal Central Asian Society*, Vol. XXVI (1939)

Mackie, J. B. 'Hasa: An Arabian Oasis', *Geographical Journal*, Vol. LXIII (1924)

Melamid, Alexander, 'Boundaries and Petroleum Developments in Saudi Arabia', *Geographical Review*, XLVIII (1957)

Melamid, Alexander. 'Oil and the Evolution of Boundaries in Eastern Arabia', *Geographical Review*, Vol. XLIV (1954)

Melamid, Alexander. 'Political Boundaries and Nomadic Grazing', *Geographical Review*, Vol. LV (1965)

Melamid, Alexander. 'Political Geography of Trucial Oman and Qatar', *Geographical Review*, XLIII (1953)

Nakhleh, Emile A. 'Labor Markets and Citizenship in Bahrayn and Qatar', *Middle East Journal* (Spring 1977)

O'Leary, Patrick. 'The Butterfly Hunter Who Found Arabia's Oil Riches', *The Times*, 16 December 1971

Parry, Capt. R. St. P. 'The Navy in the Persian Gulf', *Journal Royal United Service Institution* (London), LXXXV (1930)

Philby, H. St. J. B. 'A Survey of Wahhabi Arabia, 1929', *Journal of the Central Asian Society*, Vol. XVI (1929)

Philby, H. St. J. B. 'The New Reign in Saudi Arabia', *Foreign Affairs*, Vol. 32 (1954)

Rutter, Eldon. 'Slavery in Arabia', *Journal of the Royal Central Asian Society*, Vol. XX (1933)

Said, Rosemarie J. 'The Conflict Over The Arab Islands in the Gulf, 1918-1971' (in Arabic), *Journal of the Gulf and Arabian Peninsula Studies*, II No. 6 (1976)

Standish, J. F. 'British Maritime Policy in the Persian Gulf', *Middle East Studies*, Vol. 3, No.4 (1967)

Thomas, Bertram. 'Arab Rule Under the Albusaid Dynasty of Oman 1741-1937', The Raleigh Lecture on History, *Proceedings of the British Academy*, Vol. 24 (London, 1938)

Toynbee, Arnold (ed.). 'The Dispute Between Persia and Great Britain Over Bahrain (1927-1934)', *Survey of International Affairs* (1934)

Toynbee, Arnold (ed.). 'The Rise of the Wahhabi Power' and 'The Delimitation of Frontiers', *Survey of International Affairs* (1925), Vol. 1 (1927)

Wahba, Hafiz. 'Wahhabism in Arabia', *Journal of the Central Asian Society*, Vol XVI (1929)

Wilkinson, J. C. 'The Oman Question: The Background to the Geography of South-East Arabia', *Geographical Journal*, CXXXVII (1971)

Wilson, Sir Arnold Talbot. 'A Periplus of the Persian Gulf', *Geographical Journal*, LXIX (1927)

6. Newspapers

Umm al-Qura, Mecca
Al-Ahram, Cairo
Al-Anwar, *Al-Nahar*, Beirut
Cuttings from the British and French presses available at the Press Archives, Royal Institute of International Affairs, London
Financial Times
Guardian

7. Journals

Middle East Economic Digest, London, 1969-78

INDEX